Going Deep

My Transcendent Journey into Theta Consciousness

Deborah Knight Eaton

BALBOA.
PRESS
A DIVISION OF HAY HOUSE

Author Credits:
Deborah has an exceptional talent for describing aptly and vividly practical guidelines for achieving a state of tranquility. You describe your out-of-body experiences as very real happenings. You are an exceptional healer.

Balboa Press books may be ordered through booksellers or by contacting:

Balboa Press
A Division of Hay House
1663 Liberty Drive
Bloomington, IN 47403
www.balboapress.com
1 (877) 407-4847

Print information available on the last page.

ISBN: 978-1-5043-3488-4 (sc)
ISBN: 978-1-5043-3489-1 (e)

Library of Congress Control Number: 2015909974

Balboa Press rev. date: 07/24/2015

Contents

Forward

I am a researcher on a treasure hunt to find ways to take care of my own health challenges. That hunt has become my life path and my service to others who want to take charge of their own health. Recently my hunt led me to a fascination with understanding brain waves and how to induce deep states of consciousness. I learned that certain brain wave frequencies support healthy neurotransmitters, the happy hormones. These neurotransmitters affect mood, sleep, and pain levels. I wanted to find a way to control and sustain my happy serenity and get a good night's sleep. I was seeking a way to find quick access to the inner peace I associated with deep meditation.

I was interested in learning how to intentionally achieve theta brain waves which are associated with deep levels of meditation, creativity, and spiritual experiences. I experimented with brain entrainment technologies and felt some pleasant effects but knew there was something more to be discovered in the sweetness of theta.

So when Deborah invited me to experience a guided journey into theta consciousness, I agreed. Deb is my sister and I have witnessed her impeccable intuition all our lives. I have seen how she has attracted profound connections and deep healing experiences because she has always listened to her inner knowing. I trust her absolutely.

I found it easy to allow Deb to guide me into my inner awareness. She didn't tell me what to notice or experience but skillfully supported my deepening relaxation. During the relaxation experience, I was in a wooded grove by a stream, sitting in a camping chair with a book in my hands. I could see a camping van parked nearby just past a picnic table. I thought I must be in Oak Creek Canyon north of Sedona, Arizona…a favorite place.

I simply allowed the sound of the water bubbling over the rocks to nourish my inner being. This was my heaven on earth.

I have not forgotten that peace by the wooded grove, by the stream. It came to me at a time when I was searching for an answer to a big question in my life – where should I live? I am comforted with knowing I have a place that is my natural habitat. I have it in the etheric realm and I have it as a beacon on my travels. I have bought myself a motor-home to fulfill a lifelong dream and I am making that theta vision a reality. There are many bubbling streams trickling through campgrounds in our beautiful country and my theta vision has inspired me with the courage to visit my natural habitats.

Whether I am by a trickling stream or in my urban apartment, I now have the path to theta relaxation and its gift of inner peace. I just follow the simple instructions in Deborah's book. I absolutely trust the guidance from the well of theta.

With love, Judith Knight

Introduction

I've had a prayer practice for many years now. It's natural for me to pray for the people I love — family members and friends. A couple of months ago, my sister asked me a favor: She had a client in her health practice who was in a lot of pain and could I pray for her? The woman had been to several health practitioners, and for the past year she had been in agonizing pain. I agreed to help. I was given the age and name of the woman.

The next day, my sister called back and said that her client was out of pain and felt happy for the first time in a while. That's just what I like to hear. My sister asked what I did when I prayed. I decided to write her a full detail of what I do and how long I do it. After she read the routine she called with great amazement.

"Deb, I've known you all these years, and this is how you pray? I had no idea!" Her reaction of amazement gave me the nudge I needed to write this short book about what I do. Here's my story.

Since childhood, I have had out-of-the-ordinary experiences that have shaped my life and career. The first experience I had was sitting under a tree.

I think I was fortunate to grow up in the rural countryside of Maine and be able to spend a lot of time in nature. During the school year, I lived with my mom and dad and three siblings in a large white farmhouse with a red barn attached. Then in the summer, we went to live at a camp on a pond that has been in my dad's family since the late 1700's. It was wonderful to swim and run and make bonfires and learn how to paddle a canoe in the summertime and then return to the big farmhouse for the rest of the year.

The farmhouse was surrounded by white pine trees, the official tree of Maine. One of these trees was my favorite, and as a child I spent many hours sitting underneath it, making up songs about faraway places. Those precious times of gazing up at the stars, making up songs, and singing out loud began my lifelong rapport with nature. At this early age, I *knew* there was something special up there in space.

One evening, around dusk, something out of the ordinary happened — one of the stars that I had been singing to, moved towards me, traveling through time and space, and it seemed to come inside my head. As a five year old, that seemed natural. I heard a distinct audible message. *When you get older you will travel around the world so that you will know humanity better.*

I heard that sentence as if someone was actually speaking to me. It was very clear. That was all I heard for that night, but the next evening I was right out there, sitting under the pine tree. I heard that same audible voice again. This time the message was *when you reach 40 a miracle will happen.*

I would not hear that same quality of voice inside my head for many years, not until I turned 27 years old. It was in September of 1976, and I was picking tomatoes in a garden in Maine. I was the only person around when I heard a voice in my head say, *go to California.*

Within two weeks, everything fell into place, and I was in San Diego living with my sister Judith. In my early 20's, I had lived in San Diego and studied massage therapy as well as muscle testing (Touch for Health) and reflexology. When I heard the message *go to California*, it was easy to return because I already had contacts there.

In October, about a month after I arrived, I attended an annual health symposium put on by the International Biogenic Society. Students from all over the world gathered together to hear Dr. Edmond Bordeaux Szekely talk about his life's work, the Essenes. The Professor, as he was affectionately called, had written more than eighty books on the Essenes, the most popular book was *The Essene Gospel of Peace.* I had read the book and was thrilled to know that the annual gathering was held in San Diego. A coincidence?

After the symposium, there was a potluck organized but instead of going, I decided to drive east of San Diego and visit the desert. I was on the freeway; about 10 miles from town when a very odd and mysterious spell came over me while I drove. I have read about this sort of thing happening to other people but when it happened to me, I was amazed how simple and matter-of-fact it was.

I was no longer aware that it was me driving the car; instead an inner force drove it for me. This inner force did not talk to me but rather I felt an absolute inner guidance to take the next exit off the freeway. This inner force guided me to turn left, turn right, drive on side streets all across town and bingo; I arrived at the exact place where the potluck was being held.

I parked the car, walked into the house and didn't see anyone. The dining room table was covered with potluck dishes; it all looked delicious but nobody was there. Finally, my eye caught the view out the back window and there was a group of people standing in a big circle, holding hands. Once outside, a man invited me to join them and I stepped into the circle and was there just in time to do the Essene prayer to bless the food.

I found out that the man's name was Frank and he had a friend with him, Robert, who was in a wheelchair. Frank said that he had noticed me and wanted to get to know who I was and was glad that I had decided to come to the potluck. I didn't tell him that it was not me who decided to come, rather a deep calling from within. Another coincidence?

As we talked, he told me that Robert needed someone to help him over the next three months and perhaps I could help. Robert wanted to visit many of the healing spas and hot springs in California and could I be his driver and caregiver? Frank could not do it because he was flying to England; he would be back in three months and we could meet up then. I had the impression that my destiny was connected to Frank and his friend, Robert, and I happily took the job.

One of the hot springs we visited was near Mount Shasta at the Stewart Mineral Spring's Resort where a new age teacher, Stanley Burroughs, gave a ten day seminar on his life's work, *Healing for the Age of Enlightenment*. I go into greater detail in Chapter Five.

At the end of the three months, I stopped working for Robert and began working for Frank. Over the course of the next year, it became clear that I would be helping Frank with his project: traveling around the world, visiting healing spas and teaching at new age schools. Everything fell smoothly into place. I felt buoyed up and supported from an invisible protective inner force that continuously felt right, deep within.

From 1975 to 1983, I traveled around the world with Frank and met some of the most remarkable human beings on this planet, and therefore did get to know humanity better. And, yes, at age forty a miracle did happen. I received a spiritual awakening called *shaktipat* from an enlightened master.

What I have learned from my out-of-the-ordinary experiences, from the visions I received, from the travels, and from the mentors I met and the wisdom they taught me comes the substance of this book.

I have to share what I learned and how I use this wisdom now today in my prayer practice and in my life. It pours out of me, and I must write about it.

It gives me so much joy and pleasure to write about all the things I have learned, and I sincerely hope you enjoy it too.

CHAPTER 1

Brain Waves and Theta Patterning

I think the most influential wisdom I learned in all my travels was the know-how of being able to enter into deep relaxation. I started quite early in my teens in being interested in relaxation. In 1962, I read Susy Smith's book *ESP (Extrasensory Perceptions)*, and she opened up my mind to wider possibilities. She explained that the mind had lines and barriers crisscrossing it, like a grid. When a thought was sent to us and it hit one of the lines on the grid, then the thought could not get through. Yet success happened when a thought slipped through the grid and pierced our receptive mind. Voilà! ESP occurred when the thoughts got through those barriers. Susy explained it quite simply, and I was intrigued on how to have a thought get through the grid.

I began to see my brain as an intriguing labyrinth of open and closed pathways — some thoughts made it through, and some laid buried deep within my unconscious. I had a great desire to uncover and, in a way, free the inner thoughts deep in my mind.

I was in my early 20's when I had an opportunity to put those ideas to the test. My mom helped. One day she got mad at me for something. I can't remember now what it was about, but I chose not to say anything to her, and I became quiet. Later on that day, I had a full blown sore throat, and I was curious — did I have a sore throat from the words I could not say to her? Nowadays, this would be seen as a classic mind-body disconnect

— but back then, in 1968, I was still relating to my mother the way I was raised . . . children are to be seen and not heard.

I decided to lie down, get deeply relaxed, and ask my unconscious to reveal what words I had not said to her. After a short time, the words came floating up — I sensed the words were *Mom, it's not fair for you to get mad at me for something I didn't do.*

Within an hour my sore throat was gone. I was both impressed it took such a short time and thrilled that I had been able to reach my unconscious. At that moment I became a believer in the profound power of the mind-body connection.

So what had happened between my thoughts, deep relaxation, and the mind-body connection? I think I relaxed into the deep brain waves of theta, and I had access to my unconscious mind.

Let's look at what the brain waves are. In the brain, there are four brain waves (beta, alpha, theta, and delta) that we use throughout the day and night. They range from the shortest brain wave, therefore the fastest one, all the way to the longest, or slowest, brain wave.

The fastest one, called beta, is when we are in high gear, thinking very fast, making quick decisions and most often using the fight or flight response. Beta is measured from 12 to 16 cycles per second.

Often when we are in beta we find that we just can't remember someone's name...it's just on the tip of our tongue. Then, we relax a bit, slow down, and enter into alpha, and often can remember the name. This brain wave of alpha is measured from 8 to 12 cycles per second.

One of the signs of entering into alpha is when we take a deep breath and let out a sigh of relief. Gazing off into the distance and daydreaming are functions accomplished when in alpha.

Most of the time, we are utilizing these two brain waves of beta and alpha throughout the day. The autonomic nervous system goes back and forth between beta and alpha. Beta is the dominant brain wave when the sympathetic nervous system is active – helping muscles to prepare for action. Alpha is the dominant brain wave when the parasympathetic nervous system is active — deepening the breath and overall relaxation — and processing what happened in the beta range.

Every time we go to sleep, we *fall* into deeper relaxation, and our brain waves slow down. We naturally enter the theta brain wave, a range from

4 to 8 cycles per second. This is our birthright for each and every one of us. Most of us are unconscious when we enter into theta. The body and mind are deeply relaxed, much more than in alpha, and breathing is much slower.

The next level down is in the delta brain wave, and the range is 0 to 4. To summarize:

Beta: 12–16 brain waves per second
Alpha: 8–12 brain waves per second
Theta: 4–8 brain waves per second
Delta: 0–4 brain waves per second

In a way, my mother's anger was a stimulus for me to purposefully go into deep relaxation in order to reveal what my unconscious mind was holding. I relaxed deep enough to enter into the theta brain wave realm, *and* I remained awake and alert.

That's the key: to stay conscious. While being conscious, I was able to hear what I had really wanted to say to my mother. In my mind, I said it, and a mystery happened. My sore throat vanished! I do not know how it happened.

I had experienced theta as the realm where the lines, the barriers of the grid do not exist, the way that Susy Smith described. That's right. When we enter into the theta brain wave, there are no blocks, and we are open to receiving ESP. We are open to our intuition.

We are also open to ask the unconscious mind to help us in a number of ways. In this brain wave we are most receptive to suggestions we give ourselves, like positive affirmations. This is also the brain wave where we receive the good intentions that other people send to us, as in a prayer of goodwill.

Being awake and alert while in the theta brain wave realm is a real treat. It is worth the effort to learn how to enter theta and stay awake. When we are awake and in theta, we can ask our unconscious mind to help us with a project, any project we have, and we can create a blueprint or pattern of how we want that project to actualize. We can pattern what we want and ask for help when we are in theta. I have named this process *theta patterning*.

Transforming the sore throat was the beginning of me using theta patterning. Before I go into intricate detail on how to do the process of theta patterning, I want to share how effective it can be when setting a pattern for the future. I have two examples here of theta patterning: one for my own interests and another to guide someone else.

I knew that I was traveling to London with Frank, the man I met at the symposium. I wanted to focus as much positive thought on that trip as I could. I also hoped that somehow I would meet the right people and circumstances where I could be part of a total health center, offer the bodywork that I had studied, and teach classes on a variety of wellness techniques.

I dropped into deep relaxation, went into the theta patterning process and envisioned a total health center, the way I would like to see it:

- a place where an approach to mind, body, and spirit was taught
- a place where fresh vegetables grew in healthy soil, and the public would learn how to prepare delicious meals from the organic produce
- a place where the public came for workshops about healthy living

I longed to be a part of a group of people who lived what they taught — that there is a relationship between our thoughts, our actions, and how we treat other people and in return, how they treat us. I let my imagination run free, and in the deep theta realm, I *felt* wholeheartedly that there was a place like that, and I longed to be a part of it.

Here's what happened in just three months. When Frank and I arrived in London, we lived at the Churchill Center, a school of holistic therapies that was owned and run by Frank's friend, Ken Holmes. He and I lived downstairs and gave workshops in the upstairs rooms, and I gave bodywork sessions.

A woman named Sabine came to see me, and she was impressed with the techniques I used. Sabine was the organizer of holistic conferences for the European Association for Humanistic Psychology (EAHP), and the next one she was putting together was coming up in three months in Geneva, Switzerland. She invited us to come and present a workshop.

We went, and while at the week-long conference, a woman, Noelle, attended the workshop I gave on foot reflexology. Noelle had a reflexology school in Geneva and invited us to teach at her school for a month. Noelle was another integral player in this adventure.

During that month, she introduced us to Dr. Schaller, a medical doctor *extraordinaire*. Dr. Schaller had a total health center, Fondation Soleil, in a nearby village outside Geneva. He invited Frank and me for a tour of his foundation.

There were five estates, all within walking distance of each other. The first estate was the welcoming center for people arriving from all over the world. It was a hub of activity.

The second estate was a large work-study vegetable garden and orchard, teaching the public how to grow food with the principles of the Findhorn Gardens that were so successful in northern Scotland — that nature spirits, in the unseen world, were available to offer guidance in growing produce that was healthy without the use of pesticides.

The third estate was run by Brian Clement, the man who understood Ann Wigmore's wheat grass juice cleansing regime. Brian grew the wheat grass in large trays, and taught the public how to grow a variety of sprouts. (Dr. Brian Clement and his wife Anna Marie Clement are now the owners of the famous Hippocrates Health Institute in West Palm Beach, Florida.)

The fourth estate was a library well stocked with books about health and wellness from all perspectives. At this estate, Dr. Schaller had a staff of people who translated books into many different languages. Books that the doctor had written and books written by health practitioners from all over the world were translated from their language into English or vice versa.

One of the favorite authors was the Essene professor Dr. Edmond Bordeaux Szekely. Frank and I knew the professor, and I am sure that is why Dr. Schaller invited us to live and offer our workshops at his fifth estate. We lived in the upstairs apartment overlooking an orchard.

In all five estates, there were a total of 33 people keeping the estates in full swing: gardeners, cooks, translators, therapists, and general maintenance people. One of my purposes was to talk with Dr. Schaller every Monday morning and discuss which of those people needed some help: a sore back from gardening, too much mental stress from translating and so forth. On the doctor's request, I gave bodywork sessions to individuals and taught classes on bodywork techniques.

We stayed there for six months, from April to October, then Frank and I would leave and travel to the southern hemispheres to New Zealand and Australia, then return in the spring to the Fondation.

For the next eight years, that was our routine, and I was a part of a thriving total health center, surrounded by people who loved being connected to nature and natural ways to keep our bodies, minds, and spirits healthy. It was all quite remarkable, really, and so full of grace.

All those years flowed with harmony, and I developed an even richer belief that *theta patterning* was a way I could participate and be a co-creator with my life.

The second example of theta patterning is the process when it involves someone else. It was during the six months from October to April when Frank and I were traveling in the southern hemispheres when we were invited to Perth, Australia to teach.

Frank was flying there a few days before me, so he could find the right housing. I was tired from all the traveling and wanted a place to rejuvenate. I did not tell Frank what I wanted; instead I went into deep relaxation and did the process of theta patterning. I wanted him to be able to find a place effortlessly. I asked for the following in the present tense:

- a house that is walking distance to the ocean
- a home that has arches in the doorways, giving a warm welcoming atmosphere
- a home with comfortable furniture and inspiring art
- a car for both of us to drive
- and all this within the price range that we've set for the six months

I did the process of theta patterning three separate times over the two weeks before Frank left for Perth. Remember, I did not discuss this with him. He went off to Perth on a Saturday; on Tuesday he called with a big grin in his voice.

He had gone over to the travel agency near his motel room, and when he walked up the stairs to the agency, the screen door opened, and he nearly ran into the woman coming out. After they apologized to one another, they started talking on the steps, and he found out that this woman was hiring the agency to find applicants who wanted to rent her house for the next six months. They both smiled and walked back inside the agency's office, where this woman explained that she and her husband were going to Saudi Arabia for half a year.

He went on to explain, "Oh Deborah, you'll like this house. It's two blocks from the ocean and perfect for taking walks. The rooms inside are well decorated. The couple lived overseas for years and collected art which is all throughout the house. And listen to this — arches lead from the living room into the kitchen. They're leaving their car, and we can drive it if we need to, and it's right within our price range."

You can see how fun it is to use the process of theta patterning. I have continuously used theta patterning for these past 45 years in all areas of my life: travel, sports, health, relationships, work, living locations, spiritual growth, emotional self-esteem, and an overall sense of well-being.

In the next chapter I explain my perspectives on what forces are at work, so that theta patterning can actualize. I share how I came to imbibe this theta realm and how a mentor helped in identifying it.

CHAPTER 2

Human Being, Duality, and Non-Duality

To become proficient in theta patterning, I think it is important to understand how to feel safe in deep relaxation and also how to train the mind to have positive thoughts. When we are in theta, we cannot have negative thoughts. If we do, the brain waves speed up, and we are in the alpha range.

To me that is a natural protection or safeguard while we are in theta. Therefore, from my perspective, the thoughts and beliefs we have about our life, govern our ability to remain awake and alert in the theta brain wave. I believe that this is where the theory of quantum physics comes in handy.

I think that the theory of quantum science is one of the most important realizations of our time. It opens up the understanding that the person who is doing an experiment is also the person who has an effect on the results of that experiment.

In other words, the person who looks into the microscope will see what they are intending (or ready) to see. Someone else will look into the same microscope and see a different result. This phenomenon had to be explained in the science world. When the science community announced the quantum theory, that the observer influences the observed, the meditation community understood.

We see what we are ready to see. What we notice in other people, we also have within ourselves. When the student is ready, the teacher appears. To me, the quantum theory explains the synchronicity of timing.

When I heard the message *go to California* I was ready to act on that. I was in right timing.

When I did the theta patterning for the project to be with a total health center, I was ready to meet someone like Dr. Schaller and be a part of the Fondation Soleil.

When we meditate, there is a change in our energetic vibration that affects the well-being in our minds and bodies. This change can be described as a resonating frequency with a higher vibration. This same resonance can happen when we relax deeply.

This resonance is important because when we are relaxed, we are in less stress, and we are more aware of our mind-body connection. We are more whole. This quantum theory is like a nudge to wake us up to the fact that our lives can be co-created by what we think, how we feel, and what expectations we have. We can awaken to the things that matter and have value in our lives.

This is empowering because we have the possibility to participate with the events of our own lives. We can become co-creators. As we more fully understand and interact with the quantum theory concepts, we realize that we are responsible for our *intentions* in an event.

Therefore, it empowers us to know how we feel and what we are thinking.

So many mentors have said to me *know what's in your mind*. This brings me to another one of the most important realizations of our time and that is the *unified field theory*. Briefly, what I am thinking is affecting all that is around me.

If you saw the movie *Like Water for Chocolate*, you would have watched the unified field theory all the way through the movie. The main character, the third born daughter, was forced to remain at home and tend to her mother. Well, the daughter was depressed and prepared the food, but her tears of despair fell into the soup.

When the mother ate the soup, she started to cry and became depressed.

This movie had a lot of poetic license and showed me the power of emotions. What mood am I in when I prepare food? How does my emotional body affect me and others? I always like eating in a restaurant that has a happy chef!

I have learned that what we *feel* has an influence on others — not just the immediate family — our mood can affect people and animals and plants from far away.

When the owner of potted plants has to leave those plants in Tokyo and flies to Los Angeles, the plants respond at the precise moment when the owner thinks of them.

The unified field theory helps us become more aware that we are all connected. An example is when a prayer is offered for someone: The prayer becomes a positive intention and is felt by the person receiving the prayer.

Remember that after I received the message *go to California* everything flowed for me to get to San Diego. When I heard that message out in the garden in Maine, I immediately walked into the house and phoned my sister Judith. When I asked her for a few hundred dollars so I could fly west, she said absolutely because on that very day, she had received the $14,000 from the bank. Her house had been sold, and escrow had gone through.

To me, that timing was an example of the unified field theory! I felt something, acted on it, and it all fell into place. I think that it all stemmed from the message I received as a young girl, sitting under the pine tree.

I think that the more we understand the quantum and the unified field theories, it can help us accept ourselves and begin to accept the out-of-the-ordinary experiences that we have.

It is us *being* us. And what are we? We are human beings. Right there, in our description of ourselves, we have the holistic concept. The *human* part is our personal identification, our name, personality, our pride of ownership, how we express our ego, and how we save face. It is also the part that makes us feel separate from another.

But wait — we have a whole other part of our nature, the *being* part, and this is our lifesaver because it always holds the truth for us — that we are always in a constant stream of consciousness and absolutely connected with everything. We feel it as unconditional love.

I like to explain a *human being* this way: The *human* is in the realm of duality — and the *being* is in the realm of non-duality.

Duality requires that there is a reference to another... of anything. When you say you feel good, you need to have the feeling of bad to use as a reference — otherwise there would be no description of why something was good... or cold... or sweet or soft or better. Compared to what?

When we compare ideas, lifestyles, compare me to you, us to them, our group to their group, we are using references that exist in the dualistic world. We are human, and it has to be this way.

In duality there are two parts, just like the cell structure of life on Earth. One part of the cell is positive, the other negative. This tug of push-pull qualities is what gives us this materialistic and physical world, and is what gives us our passion for competition. Competition is and can be exciting. It gives us great aspirations to strive towards a goal... what is that goal?

One of the goals is to find harmony within ourselves — to finally have inner peace, to drop deep into our center so that we can find stillness. One of the human frustrations is that we cannot find this goal of inner peace with the duality realm. We must let go and leap into non-duality.

Non-duality is the realm we enter when we fall deep asleep. We also can enter into it through meditation and contemplation in a state of self-realization. We can enter into non-duality through great physical exertion, called the zone. We can also enter into it through deep relaxation.

The non-duality realm is all around us, all through us. It is everywhere at all times and is an infinite sphere of consciousness. This is also known as the unified field I wrote about earlier. Some people refer to non-duality as awareness, as consciousness and as the Self.

It can be described as being detached (or neutral) from an opinion about someone or an event. That's actually one way we can discern if we are in the non-duality realm... we think of a stressful event and wait... if we remain relaxed and continue to have stillness, then we most likely are in the non-duality realm.

This helps the autonomic nervous system to be in good balance. It's like floating in an energy field of endless possibilities where everything is okay, everything is all right. We don't need anything, because we already have everything. We are connected in a profound way.

What I love so much about human beings is that we do *know*, consciously or unconsciously, that we are all connected. We do *know* that there is more to us than meets the eye. We feel this connection with our pets, when we are in nature, when we moved by art.

This *knowing* is always present, but we cannot touch it or pin it down. It's a feeling that we can use and can learn how to dwell in it, and the feeling is unconditional love. Love without a reference. Love without a reason. I love you just because you are you.

I came to understand this through a spiritual experience I had in 2013. I was with my sister, Judith, on a business trip to Long Beach, California.

We were taking a short break in our hotel room, and we had to be back at the conference center in about an hour and a half.

I bent over to take off my shoes when a sharp pain shot through my left side. I had recovered from pancreatitis and Lyme disease earlier that year, and I was so bummed out to feel the pain again. Judith heard me groan, was concerned, and sat down opposite me on the other bed.

I started to moan and groan, and told her about the pain in my side. Judith guided me through a whole series of tapping — a system where you tap the acupuncture points on your head, face, and arms to bring about a neutral response to emotional and physical pain.

As I tapped from the top of my head all the way down my face and out my arm, I continued to cry out all my thoughts and emotions, and it turned into a rage against the unfairness of it all. I turned this rage against God, and in between my tears and anger I yelled, "God, it's not fair! I can't take this pain anymore. You made a mistake! You got the wrong person. Why me?"

The extreme measure of those outbursts was stronger than I had ever felt before. All the while, Judith was watching me, and right after I yelled at God, she could see a transformation happen on my face.

What I experienced was as if I was squeezed through the thin space in an hour glass, and I popped out into another dimension. From the rage I fell into complete calmness. All I could see was the color of deep cobalt blue with little sparkles of light flickering here and there. I was in awe of the majestic infinite space.

I think my words were "Wow!" On my right cheek I felt a soft touch and noticed that a large head was pressing on my cheek. It felt divine and other-worldly.

It was a kind, benevolent, loving face, and he was coming from another dimension. He pressed his round cheek softly against my cheek, rounded his lips and blew a stream of breath out of his mouth. The breath went right by my eyes and kept on moving. I could see it as a stream of scintillating breath.

It went out into the space of the cobalt blue and continued on and on. There was no beginning or end. We were all one. I had no pain anywhere, and everything I saw, everything I heard was magical. All I could do was smile and say *yes, of course, I love you.*

I turned towards my sister and smiled. I felt deep love for her. My eye caught the pattern on the fabric of the bedspread, and I put my hand on it.

"Wow. What a beautiful pattern." I looked around the room and felt giddy. "Wow, Jude, I feel so different."

Judith and I sat quietly for a moment, and she was just as moved as I was. We had been through something extraordinary. She realized that I was in a different time and space.

She looked at her watch and said "Oh dear, we have to be back at the conference center in 30 minutes. We'd better get ready."

"Oh Jude, what do I wear? I don't think I can dress myself."

Judith went over to the closet, took out some clothes, and handed them to me. We dressed for the evening, went out to her car, and drove the four miles to the center.

As we drove along, I looked at the houses and buildings of Long Beach, and said, "Oh Jude, look at all these wonderful buildings. People are happy here, and they can have a good life. I am so happy for them. Oh look, there is a woman walking her dog. I can just tell she's happy."

Judith turned to me and said, "Wow, Deb, you really are stoned. I'll keep an eye on you when we get there. It might be best not to talk to anyone."

"Okay, Jude." We pulled into the parking lot, and as I opened up the car door, I marveled at everything I saw. The entrance to the center was like walking into an *Alice-in-Wonderland* scene. The tall ferns and philodendrons along the pathway were spectacular. I stopped and showed Judith how miraculous they were: One side of the leaf was magenta, and the other was green. Everything was magnified.

The large entrance door was made out of oak wood, and I touched the door, feeling all the carvings on it. Then the door was opened by a hostess. She was about 19 years old and a beautiful young woman. I walked towards her, ready to say *hi, you are so beautiful,* when Judith pulled my hand and said, "We're going this way!" I was in a world of splendor. We found the room for the meeting, and there were about 30 people there. Tables were set for an evening meal.

Five people were going to be honored for all the good business they had done over the past year. I was one of the five.

The host for this meeting walked over to Judith and me. The way he walked towards us seemed totally appropriate for he had his hands held out, like I had seen drawings of Jesus holding his hands out. I walked towards him, took both his hands in mine, and said how glad I was to be there. We gazed into one another's eyes and smiled. It seemed so natural to me.

Judith found our place sittings, sat me down, and told me not to go anywhere or talk to anyone. I could barely stop from giggling.

The first woman to be honored stood up and talked for about ten minutes about how great the company was, how much help she had received from her boss in doing her sales, and she thanked everyone. She sat down, and then my name was called.

I looked at Judith, and she gave me encouragement, "You'll be fine. Just be yourself."

I went up to the front of the room and stood there for a few seconds. I put my hands on my hips, the way my grandmother used to do, pigeon-toed my feet, and said in my thickest Maine accent, "Hi there, I'm from Maine, and my grandmother used to say when you've got somethin' to do, do it well. When you've got somethin' to say, say it fast."

Everyone laughed. Well, I started to talk about Maine and told a few stories. Everyone kept on laughing, and in a few minutes I sat down. I did not say one word about business.

The rest of the evening flowed along easily. I was able to talk to people and found myself always being kind, gentle, and most of all, a warm loving feeling came out of me. I felt wonderful. This high state lasted several weeks, and it was easy to find the humor in the *human* part of human being.

At the same time, I was curious about what had happened to me. I had read about the breath coming out of an enlightened being and knew it was full of grace. I also knew that the cobalt blue color was thought to be the essence of our soul, called the blue pearl, or the Self. I had a deep knowing that I had witnessed the breath of God. I had met true divinity.

I returned to Maine, and soon thereafter I heard about a man who was giving a seminar on the works of Ken Wilbur, called The Levels of Consciousness. I was familiar with Wilbur's work and was eager to meet the man giving the talk.

As I listened to him, I knew he understood a mystical experience. His name was David Peloquin, a kind man, whose warmth and humor lightened up his talk on consciousness. David had a sparkle of mirth in his eyes, and with a light step he seemed not to take himself too seriously.

He taught the seminar from his *being*. I was thrilled to hear him explain Jung and Joseph Campbell along with Lao Tzu, and bring in Cynthia Bourgeault along with his favorite, Ken Wilbur.

I trusted David and wanted to talk to him, one-on-one, so I arranged a time when I could go and see him. It took about an hour to drive to his home, and I found the long dirt road that wound through the woods and ended up at his large log cabin. The parking area was quite large, and there were other cars there, too. A meeting place.

I was a bit early, so I strolled around outside and was drawn over to the embankment overlooking a large lake. It was beautiful to see the sparkling water reflecting the light through the tall pines. It was in the middle of May, and there was a stand of lady slipper's — five of them, then another patch, then all around the side of the hill at least 100 pink lady slippers cascaded down the hillside almost to the water's edge. Had I entered into the world of fairies and nature spirits? It was like entering into a special magical world.

I turned towards the log house, climbed up the large stepping stones and found the side door. It looked like a hobbit's house with colorful pots filled with flowers with stones and shells artistically placed around the base. I felt so welcomed and reached my hand up to ring the set of chimes over the door.

A few seconds later, David answered, and as I walked in I saw a magical world. My eyes fell upon weavings on the wall, rugs draped over the bannister, and an art table right in the middle of the kitchen. There were spices in jars and bowls filled with colorful dried fruits and bowls of teas on the counter space. There was joy everywhere. Creativity had found its home and expressed itself through the people who lived here. I didn't see David's wife, yet I could feel the touch of her spirit everywhere.

Cups of tea were made, and David led the way into a large library where the walls were lined with shelves of an assortment of books intermingled with small wooded statues of animals. Tapestries were draped over the sofa. We sat on two large overstuffed chairs that faced one another on one side of this grand room. Way down at the far end was a floor-to-ceiling stone fireplace with baskets of dried flowers on either side. Color, warmth, texture, nature, and a spell of peace and quiet invited tranquility into this place.

And so we started our three hour conversation. We had all the time in the world. I told David about the mystical experience I had earlier that spring, about the being who put his face up against my cheek and blew breath out of his lips — and then the unconditional love I felt after that. I said that I felt it was the breath of God. I also shared the prophecy I had received as a child when I sat under the pine tree.

After I finished talking, David leaned forward and said "I know why you are able to have this type of experience... you live in waking theta."

He said it so absolutely. I knew what he meant by theta, but what did he mean by waking theta?

"Waking theta?" I asked him. "You mean my brain waves stay in theta even when I am going through my day's activities?"

"Yes," David responded. "If you were in beta and/or alpha brain waves most of the time, you wouldn't be able to have the many experiences you have had. It's because you can *drop* into theta and remain there even while you are walking around, awake, that you have these experiences."

He went on to explain that in April, I had had a glimpse of the non-dual reality where there is no me, no you; no us, no them; no here, no there; no up, no down. The idea of good and bad does not mean anything. All life... *is*... and all time exists... *now* .

Thank you so much, David!

The next chapter offers scripts, so you can practice entering into theta patterning and learn how to actualize your intentions and begin the co-creation process of your own life. I certainly hope you can.

CHAPTER 3

How to Do Theta Patterning

Remember that we enter into theta every time we fall asleep, so there is a *knowing* of this realm, somewhere inside all of us. We feel relaxed, and our mind is thinking more slowly. There is no opposition to anything.

It is like looking at the blue sky, and our comment would be neutral, *Oh look at the blue sky.* There would be no evaluation of the sky being blue; it would just be blue, and we would not compare it to any other time. Also, when we thought of someone's name or of an event, we would feel love and/or joy, and there would be no judgment of good or bad. The person in our thoughts just *is*; the event just *is*.

This is what it is like to be aware, awake and alert in the realm of theta. We are in the present moment, and we feel that everything is all right.

Another way to recognize when we are in the theta realm is to have the sensation of a buzzing all throughout the body. It is a highly charged vibration of scintillating life force that is dynamic and fills us with pure energy, pure joy. Waves of electromagnetic energy pour down into our heads and flow down throughout our body, exiting our feet only to recycle around our body and enter into the top of our head again; this is repeated over and over again.

So how do we get to that realm — the theta brain wave — and remain awake and alert?

I have written three levels of relaxation exercises to help you find your way into your theta realm. When you are new to deep relaxation, the beginning script may be of some help. This first script is divided into

19

three phases to help you become familiar with going deep and the 3 *2 *1 relaxation method. Even if you are familiar with deep relaxation, read the beginning script so that you will know how to use this method. Then go ahead and follow along with the intermediate or advanced script. These are the scripts that I have found to be helpful for myself and for other people. I hope they can help you too.

Beginning Script

Begin slowly, repeat these exercises often, and within a short time you will be able to relax with complete success and confidence.

The regular text is what you are doing, inwardly.

The italics is what you are saying quietly, inwardly.

Phase 1:

1. When you go to bed tonight, lie on your back, feel the mattress underneath you, and allow your back to soften into the mattress.

2. Begin by saying to yourself, *I am so happy to be a person. Thank you for giving me this life. Thank you, whoever is listening, for allowing me to have this experience of a human being. Thank you so much. I am so glad to be born and have this life.*

3. Repeat saying *thank you* until your lungs take a natural deep breath. It will feel like a sigh, and you will notice that you relax a little bit more into the mattress.

4. At this point it is a good idea to give your mind an image to think of that will connect this feeling of relaxation that you have right now, so that when you are doing this again you can recall the image and become as relaxed as you are now.

5. One way to do that is to think of the number 3, three times. Do that now. Think of a shape that is the number 3. It can be a wooden shape or a decorative flower or perhaps a cast iron symbol of the number 3. Choose your number 3 now and think of the number 3 three times, knowing that when you think of the

number 3 three times, you will become as relaxed as you are right now. Over time you will become even more relaxed.

6. Do this a second time: Think of the number 3 three times. Let your body settle down deep into the mattress, feeling how inviting it is to have your whole body simply fall into the mattress.

7. Now, for the third time, think of the number 3 three times. When you think of the number 3 three times you will easily become as relaxed as you are now. You did a good job.

8. That's enough for tonight. Repeat this simple exercise every night until you feel very comfortable while doing it. Now you can go ahead and fall asleep.

Phase 2:

1. When you go to bed, lie on your back, say a quiet *thank you,* and allow yourself to relax into the mattress, just like you did the other nights.

2. Think of the number 3 three times. As you begin relaxing, one by one recall all the things that happened to you today. Go over each one, and allow the feelings to come up to the surface.

3. If you remember something that makes your body get tight, then feel the mattress underneath you and let your body feel the support of the mattress. Relax as much as you can and say *thank you* to whomever (to God, to your Higher Self, to your Soul) for allowing yourself to have a life.

4. Feel grateful for all the feelings you have and feel appreciation and love in your body. The mattress under you is offering support right now. Allow that support to hold you, dearly, with tenderness and love.

5. Say *thank you* for having feelings and that you have a life.

6. Say *thank you* that you are a human being, and you are glad to be alive. Again, go over the events in your day, saying thank you for having a life, and feeling the mattress as support underneath you.

7. Say a quiet *thank you* over and over again, until you can relax into the mattress.

8. When you have taken a deep breath, and you feel comfortable about thinking about your day and you remain relaxed, you are now connected with your body and mind. This is very beneficial and helps you be more at ease.

9. To help you connect to this level of relaxation again the next time you do this, it is a good idea to think of a symbol.

10. Just like you thought of the number 3 three times, think of the number 2 three times, and this will reconnect you to this ease between your body and your mind.

11. Think about the number 2 three times, knowing when you think of the number 2 three times you will be more at ease in your mind and body. You did a good job.

12. Repeat the Phase 2 exercise (preferably every night before going to sleep) until you can comfortably recall the day's events, remain relaxed, and feel a thank you in your heart. This could be a month from when you began learning how to relax or it could be just a week. You will know your right rhythm and right timing.

When you recall your day's events, and you can feel them and remain calm and relaxed in your bed, with the comfort of being wrapped in a feeling of love, then you are ready for the next phase.

Phase 3:

1. When you go to bed tonight, lie down and feel the mattress underneath you. Think of the number 3 three times and feel your body becoming more and more relaxed.

2. Now think of the number 2 three times, knowing your mind and body are at ease. Give a sigh of gratitude that you can rest and be held by love all around you. Recall your day and know the events that happened to you are just events. There is a space between you and the events. You are neutral to them, and you remain in relaxation.

3. Now, think about a small airplane, lifting off the ground and flying higher and higher into the air. Think about you being on that plane, and you are lifting up and over the ground, leaving

behind all the events of your day. The events are down there, away from you, and you are lifting up away from them.

4. Look out the window of the plane and see all the sky around you — everywhere is clear light blue sky. There is all this space around you. You are completely surrounded by space.

5. If you want, anytime, you can open your eyes, see where you are, and feel the mattress underneath you. You are still here, in bed, and you are also thinking that you are up high in an airplane. You can be in both places — one in physical reality and one in the imaginary realm. Repeat this exercise nightly until you feel completely comfortable in being in these two places at the same time.

6. Now, one night you decide to explore the other direction. Instead of going up in an airplane, you explore going underneath you. Feel the mattress underneath you, and now become curious and think what the mattress looks like inside it.

7. Think about what's even below the mattress. Think about going under the floor, under the house, down into the ground. Can you smell the ground? Can you see the foundation of your house? Now, move on down even lower into the ground. All the way down until you feel space around you, like a large open space under the ground.

8. Whenever you feel like it, you can always open your eyes and see where you are — safe and sound in bed. When you are ready, close your eyes and think about the open space under the ground.

9. Look around, and there may be large boulders, a large ledge perhaps, or maybe an underground cave. Somewhere in this space is a perfect spot for you to sit, with your legs dangling over the edge and a boulder to put your back up against and gaze around.

10. Over the next several days and as many weeks as you need, repeat this exercise until you feel safe and secure in thinking about being up in the air, or about being underground or alternating between them.

11. When you are up in the air inside the airplane you can see space all around you — the events of the day are below you.

12. When you are deep inside the earth, you can see and feel the space all around you, and the events of your day will be above you, up on top of the surface. These two places are very good ways to begin your process of learning how to relax deeply.

13. When you feel confident that you have settled into these exercises, you can at this point think of the number 1 three times knowing that when you see the number 1 three times you will be as calm, as relaxed, as safe and feeling as loved as you are right now.

14. Your mind, body, and spirit are now all in alignment. And always, every time you lie down on your mattress, quietly say *thank you* for being born, and feel the love warming your heart. You did a good job.

Intermediate Script

The following is a guided journey to strengthen your self-esteem. This prepares you for the advanced focused relaxation.

The regular text is what you are doing, inwardly.

The italics is what you are saying quietly, inwardly.

1. Before you start, take the phone off the hook and/or turn off your cell phone. Have a glass of water, and remove any tight clothing. Lie down, cover yourself with something to keep you warm, and decide if you want a pillow or not; try both with and without and choose which way allows you to relax more deeply.

2. Begin with this statement of protection:

    I am a human being.

    I am a human with a personality and an ego, and I live in this material world.

    I am also a being who knows that there is more to me than meets the eye.

    It is my birthright to experience awareness in the infinite realms of this known and unknown realm of being.

    I invoke the power of love and wisdom of my whole human being to guide me into relaxation so I may learn, so I may widen my understanding, so I may live in balance, and so I may send my help and assistance to others.

    I enter into this relaxation knowing that I am surrounded by love, and I am grateful.

    Thank you (Higher Self, Great Spirit, God).

3. Close your eyes, and allow the back of your head to fall into the mattress.
4. See the number 3 three times.
5. See the number 2 three times.
6. See the number 1 three times.
7. You are now deeply relaxed and ready to go more deeply.

8. Think about your forehead and allow it to widen, allowing a softness to form along the front of your face.

9. Allow the space between your eyebrows to widen — your eyes soften, deep inside.

10. The space around your nose widens, even the space around your mouth begins to soften and slowly widen.

11. Everything in your body begins to fall away, and you enjoy the sensation of the mattress holding up your body.

12. There is a small space between your muscles and your entire skeleton and this space begins to widen.

13. Your body takes a deep breath as you fall even more deeply into the mattress.

14. Each time you take a deep breath and have a natural sigh, you are falling deeper and deeper into the realms of relaxation. You find that you are able to focus very clearly with your mind, and you like this. You are enjoying this time of relaxation.

15. Now, take a deep breath and begin this guided journey.

16. Imagine, or think about, going down a staircase that leads you down into a cave. You can feel the cool air on your face as you go down the staircase.

17. As you reach the bottom of the staircase, you notice that there is a boat that is on the banks of a river. Move on over to the boat, get in, get comfortable, and glide out into the slow moving river.

18. You are now leaving the cave, and you glide out into the daylight. You are gliding past tall grasses that grow along the banks of the river, and you can hear the chirping of birds.

19. Now come to a bend in the river and arrive at a sandy beach. Allow the boat to come up on the sand, get out of the boat, and walk towards a meadow. In the middle of the meadow, there is a tree; go sit under it for a while. When your body takes a deep breath, you will be ready to continue.

20. In the distance there is a mystical mountain that has an entrance at its base. Go to this entrance and go inside the mountain. There is a path winding its way up to the top of the mountain. When you reach the top, climb out onto a large platform.

21. Think about all your imaginary and real life friends, and invite them to the platform on top of the mountain. When they arrive, stand up on a tall rock in the middle of your friends. They look at you, and together in unison they say to you:

    You are strong. You are capable. We all love you. You are important.
    You are a human being, and you are precious. Your life is sacred.
    It is a blessing you were born.
    You are a human being, and you are loved by all of us here on top of this mountain.
    We all love you and are so glad that you are here, to share a life experience with us.

22. Now you can make a declaration:

    Hello, hear ye, hear ye. I am a human being, and I am strong.
    I know who I am, and I feel good about myself.

You hear applause from all the people who are there on top of the mountain.

    I am full of goodness and kindness.
    I am a human being, and I am full of love.

You hear more applause, and it feels like golden sunshine pouring down on you.

    I am a human being, and I receive love from everyone.
    I am connected to all life.
    I am a human being, and I am strong.

23. Now, you feel all the love coming from this group of loved ones. Allow the love to seep into every cell in your body. Stand here for as long as you like, feeling the love being absorbed.

24. You can smell the fresh air, feel the sweet wind caressing you, and be in this vast expansive place on top of the mountain. Take it all in.

25. If you wish, you can repeat seeing the number 3 three times, the number 2 three times, and the number 1 three times. This will make it all the easier when you return to this inner level of relaxation.

26. When you are ready, take your time to slowly go back down the mountain, through the meadow and to the sandy beach. Find the boat and glide back inside the cave. Walk up the staircase and now find yourself back where you started — safe and sound in your bed.

27. Take a deep breath, stretch, open your eyes. You did a good job.

You have learned one approach on how to go into deep relaxation and focus your mind. Now you are ready to do the theta patterning.

Advanced Script

Phase 1:

Let's use this session so that you have the possibility of a good vacation and travel routine. Okay? Sounds good to me.

I use this kind of theta patterning every time I travel. Sometimes when I do this, I can go deep into focused relaxation in about ten minutes; sometimes it takes an hour.

The regular text is what you are doing, inwardly.

The italics is what you are saying quietly, inwardly.

1. Before we start, take the phone off the hook and/or turn off your cell phone. Have a glass of water, and remove any tight clothing. Lie down, cover yourself with something to keep you warm, and decide if you want a pillow or not; try both with and without, and choose which way allows you to relax more deeply.
2. Begin with this statement of protection:

I am a human being.

I am a human with a personality and an ego, and I live in this material world.

I am also a being who knows that there is more to me than meets the eye.

It is my birthright to experience awareness in the infinite realms of this known and unknown realm of being.

I invoke the power of love and wisdom of my whole human being to guide me into relaxation so I may learn, so I may widen my understanding, so I may live in balance, and so I may send my help and assistance to others.

I enter into this relaxation knowing that I am surrounded by love, and I am grateful.

Thank you (Higher Self, Great Spirit, God).

3. Always begin with a prayer. Here is an example of a prayer I use, and one you may like to use as well:

   Dear Father, Mother, God… please hear me. I am calling out to you, and I need help.
   Would you please help me?
   I am so grateful for all the help you give me, and I so appreciate being with you.
   Thank you so much. I am here. Please hear me.
   I need help. Please Jesus, please Buddha, please Mother Mary, please Mary Magdalen, please Bhagawan Nityananda, please Gurumayi, please Dalai Lama, please all Great Beings of love and grace, please hear me.

4. As you call out the Great Beings' names, notice which ones come to mind easily and quickly. As they approach, call out their names and ask to have their council.

   Hello dear Jesus. I love you.
   I feel you deep within me.
   Thank you so much for being here.
   I am so grateful, and I pull you into me.
   I feel your presence, and I fall into your love.
   I am surrounded by you, dear beloved Jesus, and I love being with you. I bless you with all my heart.

5. Now let yourself fall below the space where you are. If in bed, fall under the bed and go down through the floorboards and under the ground, then deeper into the earth.

   a. Or you may choose to lift up to the ceiling, feel light and weightless, and float above the earth. Feel your whole body quiver with scintillating waves of light with a high vibrational frequency. Feel waves of soft love quivering throughout your cells.

6. You are in the theta realm. Now that you are in this realm, begin talking with the Great Being(s).

   Dear Father, Mother, God.
   I am going on a trip, and I am asking for your protection.
   I ask that the flight be well organized.
   I ask that it is with ease, comfort, and joy that I am taken to a hotel that is perfect for my needs.
   I would like a hotel that is clean, is full of kind people, and within the price range that is good for me.
   I would like to stay about one block away from the center of town and be able to buy food at the local farmer's market.
   I ask that this whole trip be surrounded with love. I ask that the taxi driver know where to go.
   I ask you to help me meet the right people and have help if I need it.

7. After you think you have mentioned all you wish to ask, then, with great feeling, the biggest feeling you have, FEEL love, FEEL gratitude, FEEL totally one with all, and once again, bring to the front of your mind your wishes and what you are asking.

8. Now, streamline those wishes into a symbol, like a stream of light or a big rose or rays of sunshine or waves of aurora borealis. Over and over again, about 30 times, streamline what you are asking, and become absorbed in a sea of undulating vibrational frequency.

9. Allow your personality to disappear and become a stream of energy. With this strong feeling, you are making a new blueprint, a new pattern, and you are feeling it as if it is already happening.

10. After you have streamlined the wishes into theta patterning, lie peacefully and do not use your mind for anything. Just relax and go blank. Slowly, begin to float back to present time; feel a click, like a soft subtle re-entering of your body.

11. If you wish, you can say a farewell.

    Thank you so much, Dear Father, Mother, God. I am so happy to be with you.
    I love you. Bye.

12. Now get up, wash your face, have a drink of water. If you need to, have some nuts or even a small piece of chocolate. A meditation master once told me that chocolate was the great grounding food after being in another realm.

Phase 2:

When you wish to send a beneficial intention of goodwill to someone else, here is an idea of a script for theta patterning. It is very similar to Phase 1, and you can substitute the fictitious name of Mary Smith for your person, or animal, for the session. The time varies according to how long it takes for you to enter into theta. Some days you may be able to enter into theta in about ten minutes; sometimes it may take an hour.

The regular text is what you are doing inwardly. *The italics is what you are saying quietly, inwardly.*

1. Before you start, take the phone off the hook and/or turn off your cell phone. Have a glass of water, and remove any tight clothing. Lie down, cover yourself with something to keep you warm, and decide if you want a pillow or not; try both with and without, and choose which way allows you to relax more deeply.
2. Begin with this statement of protection:

I am a human being.
I am a human with a personality and an ego, and I live in this material world.
I am also a being who knows that there is more to me than meets the eye.
It is my birthright to experience awareness in the infinite realms of this known and unknown realm of being.
I invoke the power of love and wisdom of my whole human being to guide me into relaxation so I may learn, so I may widen my understanding, so I may live in balance, and so I may send my help and assistance to others.
I enter into this relaxation knowing that I am surrounded by love, and I am grateful.
Thank you (Higher Self, Great Spirit, God).

3. Always begin with a prayer. Here is an example of a prayer I use, and one you may like to use as well:

    Dear Father, Mother, God… please hear me.
    I am calling out to you, and I need help.
    I have someone here, and I need your help with this person.
    Would you please help me?
    I am so grateful for all the help you give me, and I so appreciate being
        with you.
    Thank you so much.
    I call out for help for Mary Smith, Mary Smith, Mary Smith.
    I am here. Please hear me. I need help.
    I present Mary Smith, Mary Smith, Mary Smith. I ask for help.
    Please Jesus, please God, please Siddhas, please Buddha, please all
        Great Beings of love and grace, please hear me.

As you call out the Great Beings' names, notice which ones come easily and quickly. As they approach, call out their names and ask to have their counsel.

    Hello dear Jesus. I love you.
    I feel you deep within me.
    Thank you so much for being here.
    I am so grateful, and I pull you into me.
    I feel your presence, and I fall into your love.
    I am surrounded by you, dear beloved Jesus, and I
    love being with you. I bless you with all my heart.

4. Now let yourself fall below the space where you are. If in bed, fall under the bed and go down through the floorboards and under the ground, then deeper into the earth.

    a. Or you may choose to lift up to the ceiling, feel light and weightless, and float above the earth. Feel your whole body quiver with scintillating waves of light with a high vibrational frequency. Feel waves of soft love quivering throughout your cells. You are in the theta realm.

5. Now that you are in this realm, begin talking with the Great Being(s).

    Dear Jesus, I bring to you Mary Smith. Please show me how I can help this person.

6. Wait. Slowly, you may be able to see or sense where Mary needs balance and ease. You may see a black dark spot on her head and somehow know that she has a headache. This is the time to be receptive and allow your intuition to give you information.

7. This part of the theta patterning is spontaneous, full of feeling, and very intense with waves of energy moving through your body. At some point, usually no longer than ten minutes, proceed to the next phase and give a prayer of thanks.

    Dear Father-Mother, God.
    Thank you for helping Mary to feel better.
    Thank you for showing me what is bothering her.
    Mary's head is smooth, clear, and perfectly healthy.
    Mary's head is vibrant and fresh, and feels wide open and free.

8. Now, with great feeling, the biggest feeling you have, FEEL love, FEEL gratitude, FEEL totally one with all, and once again, bring to the front of your mind the image of Mary being absolutely well and in ease. Streamline this image of Mary into a symbol — like a big rose or see Mary surrounded by rays of sunshine.

9. Over and over again, about 30 times, streamline the healthy image of Mary and feel waves of moving energy circulating around your body.

10. Keep the image of Mary in your thoughts and pour love into her image.

11. Pour love from the heart of the Great Beings you have called upon and put all the intentional force you can muster into her image.

12. Allow your personality to disappear and become a stream of energy. With this strong feeling, you are making a new blueprint, a new pattern of Mary's head and energy field, and you are feeling it as if it is already happening.

13. After you have streamlined in theta patterning, lie peacefully and do not use your mind for anything. Just relax and go blank.
14. Slowly, begin to float back to present time; feel a click, like a soft subtle re-entering of your body. If you wish, you can say a farewell.

Thank you so much, Dear Father, Mother, God.
I am so happy to be with you.
I love you. Bye.

15. Slowly get up, wash your face, have a drink of water, and maybe a nut or a piece of chocolate. You have done a good job.

Here's something to think about: The next time you do a theta patterning session, just before you do, ask yourself these three questions:

What do I look like? Do I feel irritable?
Do I have physical pain?

After you finish a session, ask those three questions again and look into the mirror. How do you look? How do you feel, emotionally and/or physically?

If you are like me, you will almost always look softer, younger, and your face will feel smoother. I personally am more mellow and calmer, and I feel joy to be a human being. I feel balanced. My physical body feels more supple and at ease. In general, I have a heightened sense of wellness in mind, body, and spirit.

Going into theta patterning helps living in the other brain waves of alpha and beta much easier. I believe that when we are in the theta brain wave, we are in the *being* part of our divine nature. When we are in either alpha or beta, we are operating in the *human* part.

It's a win-win principle when using theta patterning, because we achieve a feeling of deep connection with our inner self, and that is glorious. Remember, we are all human beings, with a personality and an ego, along with the divine love in our hearts.

CHAPTER 4

The Temple of the Emerald Green Water

It was 1979, and the venerable teacher of the Essenes, Professor Edmond Bordeaux Szekely, had just passed away. I was in Geneva with Dr. Schaller and the staff of Fondation Soleil. The Schallers were fond of the professor, and they knew his surviving wife, Norma Jean.

Dr. Schaller held a formal meditation for the professor, and it was held in a large room where about 40 people could sit in a round circle. Norma Jean led the guided meditation and then became quiet.

I believe that the high spiritual frequencies of all those people in that room were influential in creating the atmosphere for me to be able to receive the following vision. I use the vision to this day, and I invite you to use it in any way you can. I have named it The Temple of the Emerald Green Water.

First, I'll take you through it the way I experienced it, and then I will give you a shorter description so that you can use it when you go into theta patterning.

Right after Norma Jean became quiet, I was lifted out of my body, lifted up over Geneva, and moved through time and space, and landed in the middle of a hillside. Looking up, all I could see was deep green grass rolling up the hill.

On top of the knoll was a temple all in white marble.

I drifted up the hill, floated up the wide marble stairs leading up to the temple, and walked through the open doors. I was looking down a long hallway with open doors on either side.

As I walked down the hall, I could see into the rooms, and they looked like classrooms equipped with white boards on the wall. Each room had about ten chairs in them. There were no students in the rooms, yet I did see a teacher standing at one of the white boards with a marker. The person was translucent and androgynous.

I walked into the classroom, sat down, and the teacher gave me a lesson. The white board was covered with symbols, and an algorithmic equation was put up on the board. I had no idea what it meant or what the teacher said. It went right over my head.

After a while, I left the room and walked out of the temple. As I gazed over the wide sweep of green grass, I noticed some boulders clustered near the base of the lawn. A footpath led in that direction, so I went towards them. As I approached the boulders, I could see and smell and hear a flowing river. I felt the cool refreshing spray of the water.

On my right, Pegasus, the white winged horse, appeared and bent down to drink the river water. As the horse drank, I noticed that the water had a deep green color, and Pegasus's body was filled with emerald green sparkling water.

A water ladle was nearby. A small being, like a nature spirit, picked up the ladle and scooped up some water for me. The water was indeed a deep emerald green.

I drank some, and it felt like I was filled with deep nourishment. An inner calmness came over me. I looked around and marveled at the green river, the green hillside, the natural walkway all the way back up to the temple.

I returned to the room in Geneva, full of people in meditation just as Norma Jean asked us to open our eyes and come back. I did share parts of the vision with the group and was told that the professor loved temples. They all agreed that he would have loved to hear about it.

Now when I have a client who has asked me to pray for them, whether they live nearby or far away, I drop into theta patterning, invite them to this temple, and take them down the path to the river of the emerald green water.

One of the nature spirits is always present and hands my client a ladle full of this highly charged water. Sometimes I invite them to lie down in the water, and I take the ladle and pour the green water over their foreheads. It seems to ease their minds and cleanse their thoughts.

I believe this is a way to receive vibrational nutrition, by soaking in the emerald green waters. It's like being immersed in chlorophyll.

Since 1979, I have revisited the classrooms in the temple. Occasionally, I have comprehended what the teachers were saying. I believe that as I am ready to understand a truth, then I will be able to perceive it. I believe this is the quantum theory in practice.

I think the teachings are similar to the Akashic Records (a realm where all knowledge is recorded), and it is a roadmap to the connection between the spirit and the mundane, which is the unified field theory in manifestation.

On the following page is a more concise form of this vision so that you can use it when you do your own theta patterning.

THE TEMPLE OF THE EMERALD GREEN WATER

1. In a faraway place in your mind, there is a sweep of green grass that rolls up a soft hill. On top of the knoll is a special building, like a temple, made out of marble. Wide stairs lead you up into the entrance, and when inside, there is a long hallway with classrooms on either side.

2. As you walk down the hall, you look in the rooms, and there are chairs and a whiteboard on the wall. There is a teacher standing nearby, holding a marker. The teacher is androgynous. The whiteboard is covered with symbols.

3. You decide to sit here and receive a lesson on a subject you have wanted to learn. You feel a connection with the teacher.

4. When you are ready, you can leave this place of learning. As you go outside, your gaze sees the wide sweep of green lawn. A group of boulders are clustered near the base of the lawn, and a natural footpath leads down to them.

5. As you approach, you can see and hear a river; it is so crisp and alive with sparkling water. The river is moving slowly, and you feel the cool refreshing spray of the water.

6. On your right, Pegasus appears and bends down to drink of the water in the river. As the horse drinks, you notice that the water is crystal clear with a strong emerald green color, and his body is filled with this green emerald water.

7. You see a ladle nearby and scoop up some water. The water is a deep emerald green. You drink some, and it fills you up with deep nourishment, and you become very calm.

8. You step into the river, lie down, and absorb the deep green water. It goes into your body and nourishes all parts of your cells.

9. You can come here anytime and immerse yourself in this emerald green river. The green water purifies all your cells.

10. Give thanks and return to your present time.

CHAPTER 5

Healing for the Age of Enlightenment

During those years of travel, one of the brilliant mentors I met was a man named Stanley Burroughs, the author of *Healing for the Age of Enlightenment*. It's a story I love to tell, and it will tie in to the vision of the Temple, the Emerald Green Water, and explain how color is so helpful in bringing our bodies back to harmony.

I met Stanley when he was 84 years old. When he was 29, he received a vision that showed him a series of techniques to stimulate the reflexes throughout the body, from the head all the way down to the toes. The feet had their own complete technique, which also stimulated the whole body. He named this Vita-Flex.

He also received a vision to make a lemonade drink using lemons or limes, maple syrup, and a pinch of cayenne pepper. He called this the Master Cleanser or the Lemonade Diet.

The vision included the use of color, and he put together a complete body therapy using colored gels (similar to the theatrical colored gels used in lighting the stage). For 55 years he taught that toxins were the cause of many diseases. The way back to health was to eliminate the toxins as quickly and effectively as possible. His book *Healing for the Age of Enlightenment,* explained his ideas and how to go about doing them.

The intention is to keep on the cleanse until the tongue is no longer coated. Stanley Burroughs taught that the better the elimination of toxins, the better the return to wellness. He suggested two possible approaches to elimination: a laxative herb tea or the saltwater flush. The salt water flush is the ayurvedic cleansing routine that yogis have used over hundreds of years. He suggested asking an herbalist for the correct laxative combination.

Here is a summary of his therapies:

1. A balanced-nutrition fast using the recipe called the Master Cleanser: a lemonade drink made up of 6 oz. of water, 2 Tablespoons of maple syrup, 1 Tablespoon of lemon or lime juice, and 1/8 Teaspoon of cayenne pepper.
2. Vita-Flex: a revitalization of the reflexes.
3. Color Therapy: sitting under the appropriate colored gels.
4. An herbal laxative or the Salt Flush: two level teaspoons of sea (not iodized) salt in a full quart of lukewarm water, drunk quickly in the morning on the fifth day of the Master Cleanser regimen.

His suggestion to do the salt flush is one that took daring for me to do. By the fifth day of the Master Cleanser, the bowels will have moved a majority of the buildup of fecal matter, and this salt water flush is taken to cleanse much more thoroughly. Burroughs did not suggest enemas or colonics and thought that the salt water flush was very safe and effective.

If you are planning on doing it, you might want to talk to your health provider and make sure it is safe for you to do it. It can be quite difficult to drink down the quart of salt water. I have gone on the Master Cleanser ten times and have only done the salt water flush twice. I was glad I did it, because I felt much cleaner.

Stanley has written more about this in his book, and you might want to read it from start to finish before you go on the Master Cleanser.

Stanley taught workshops at a hot springs near Mt. Shasta in northern California and also in Hawaii, his home. I was able to attend his ten day workshop at the hot springs.

The workshop was designed to prepare students to become teachers of his work, therefore all 20 of us were encouraged to go on the Master Cleanser, receive a Vita-Flex treatment every day, and spend at least one hour a day under a colored gel. I had never fasted before, so I was grateful to have the supervision and be with other people who were fasting as well.

Fortunately, there were ten health coaches to help Stanley, and with 20 students that was a good ratio, 1 to 2.

Each day, we listened to Stanley talk about healthy living. He showed us how to give the Vita-Flex treatments on the reflex points on our arms, legs, feet, and hands. I had studied reflexology before and was able to follow along. What surprised me was how tender my feet were when Stanley gave me a Vita-Flex treatment.

Every day, we were put into a hot sauna and allowed to sweat, and then wrapped in towels until we cooled down.

The color therapy was next. The room had two massage tables, and above each one was the lamp that held the colored gels. The light bulb was 150 watts, so it did not give off too much heat. The first color used was always green to bring about balance, and the treatment took about an hour. Stanley said that it took about that long for the auric body to absorb the color green and make a substantial shift.

I likened it to dry arid earth needing water so the best way is to slowly drip water onto the earth. He also encouraged us to eat lots of green foods. Depending on the individual person, the next colored gel would be the warm color of red (or yellow) or to the other side of the spectrum, a cool color of blue (or violet).

The third round of color therapy would be a combination of the primary colors, depending on each person, and the treatment would always end with green. To do a complete treatment could take up to three hours, and it could be done over a few days if that was preferred.

I was either in the sauna, soaking in a bathtub of hot sulfur water, under the colored lamp, getting a Vita-Flex treatment, or in classes with Stanley and the other students.

On the seventh day of the Master Cleanser, I was outside on the deck when a wave of nausea swept over me. I leaned over the railing and smelled the sulfur from the mineral springs, then got weak and nearly fell on my knees.

I made a mad dash to the toilet and got there just in time. From my bowels, I eliminated a thick black piece of tar that was about a foot long. It was hard, like a stick, and stank as if it were thousands of years old, like a swamp.

I was weak for a minute or two, then washed my hands and face, combed my hair, and drank a tall glass of fresh water. I was amazed how much better I felt — and so light! I felt like a swan!

I had a history of long and difficult menstrual periods. Directly after the cleansing, the difference was remarkable. My periods were regular every 28 days — the cycle of the moon — and for the next 20-plus years I experienced no noticeable PMS or cramping.

Getting rid of the thick hard piece of tar was an excellent result of all of the combined therapies Stanley offered. After the elimination, the Vita-Flex therapy did not hurt my feet at all, a very different reaction from the first day.

I do agree with the idea that toxins have to be eliminated from the body, and his whole approach has been my favorite type of a fasting cleansing regime. Often when I do go on the Master Cleanser, I include Vita-Flex, color therapy, and the salt flush.

When I come off the cleanser, I follow his instructions on how to introduce foods into the digestive system. I have found it takes as many days to come off this cleanse as to the number of days you were on it.

To determine how many days to be on the cleanse, you can use the color of your tongue as the gauge. While the body is detoxifying, the tongue is coated with a white film. When the body is finished with the cleanse, the tongue will turn a soft healthy pink.

The average amount of time I have done the Master Cleanser is nine days. I take the next nine days to gradually introduce foods back into my digestive system.

Stanley emphasized how healing the color green was — in color therapy and in eating green vegetables. Whenever in doubt, think and eat green.

I was now ready to learn more bodywork systems. In the next chapter, I will introduce Polarity Therapy.

CHAPTER 6

Polarity Therapy

I learned polarity therapy from Frank while we were traveling. Polarity therapy is the work of Randolph Stone who studied the ancient principles of Ayurveda. If you studied polarity in its entirety, you would not have to learn another therapy because of the Ayurvedic principles.

Polarity therapy teaches a bodywork system that sees the body as an electrical current, which runs all the way through it. By connecting the electrical points, the body can be brought into wellness.

It also has a cleansing system a little different than the Master Cleanser. It uses lemon juice and spices to cleanse the liver, with no maple syrup.

Polarity teaches body exercises to open up the joints, and especially squatting down to open up the hip joints. It was difficult for me to receive a polarity treatment because I could not squat. Frank put a two-by-four piece of wood underneath my heels to help make it easier, and that was still nearly impossible. My hips were so tight, and they ached terribly.

Frank worked on the electromagnetic points in my body and started getting the natural flow of electricity moving through my joints, until finally I started to have more flexibility. It took about three months for me to be able to do the squatting posture, yet once I succeeded I could do it easily. I can still do it to this day, after all these years.

The squatting exercise helps you release the tension in your back muscles up and down your spine, from the back of your head down to your coccyx. Randolph Stone learned this from people who did not sit in a chair but rather squatted on the ground to do their daily chores, like eating and reading. He noticed that their backs, legs, and hips were so much more flexible than those people who sat in chairs most of their lives.

An effective way to begin doing the squat is to wear some shoes with a slight heel, that way you can gradually open up your hips and the front of your thighs. It takes time yet is well worth the effort.

Between the elimination of the toxins and the opening up of my hip area, now I was more integrated in my body. That had a definite benefit to my whole mind-body-spirit connection.

I believe all the releases I experienced in getting rid of the toxins and the increase of flexibility in my body helped to raise my vibrational frequencies so that I could receive the visions. I also believe it has helped me to go into deep relaxation and theta patterning. I am most grateful.

I also believe that the message *go to California* was part of an overall plan. I met Frank, met the Essenes, studied with Stanley Burroughs, and learned polarity therapy.

I had already studied several systems on my own: deep relaxation, foot reflexology, and muscle testing with the system of Touch for Health. Everything had fallen into place, and I was curious if this was part of my destiny. I wondered what would happen next.

CHAPTER 7

The Fondation Soleil

During those years while I was in Geneva with the Schaller's, I attended a lecture given by R.D. Laing, the psychologist who wrote *The Politics of Experience*. I had read his book in the late sixties when I was in college and was glad to catch up on his latest ideas.

Laing was involved with the process of childbirth and the attitudes the parents had during the pregnancy. He believed there was an emotional imprint felt by the unborn child inside the womb, and it carried outward after birth.

During the lecture, I raised my hand and said that I wanted to know about the healing process especially when there has been a trauma to the person.

To answer my question, he went to the white board and drew a graph that showed the timeline of a person's life, from birth to adulthood.

"Let's say for example," he said, "that a person experienced a rather traumatic event at an early age of five years old." Laing drew a squiggly line from age five parallel to the base line. He stopped the line when it reached the same set point as the person's age, much higher on the graph.

"When a person gets older, the subtle vibration of this lower squiggly line has an influence on the person's mind and body well-being, even their emotional state.

"When the adult relaxes deeply and drops directly down from the timeline until they reach the parallel line coming over from age five, the adult is then in the same psychic vibrational imprint that the traumatic event made, so many years prior.

"It's as if the adult can revisit the trauma in deep relaxation. The adult doesn't have to go back to age 15, or 10, etc. He or she can relax deeply and make a new imprint at that level, in deep relaxation, and rebound back to the present time.

"That new imprint needs to be remade over and over again until the adult actualizes it."

Bingo!

As Laing explained this, my head was bobbing up and down because it confirmed my ideas about the value of going deep within your mind. What I got out of his answer was that I could re-pattern the past by dropping deep into relaxation with a focused mind, and erase the imprinted block.

You can see how this appealed to me. Remember, this was in 1977, and I was just formulating my ideas about wellness. I think this idea from R.D. Laing started to incubate within my creative mind.

I am so glad I asked him that question! It's often the questions we ask that open doors to our way of thinking.

I learned so many valuable lessons with the Schallers. I loved hanging out with the gardeners. Now these were not your typical gardeners. They were taught by experts in how to listen to plants; how to talk and communicate with the flowers; how to hear the vegetables give instructions on what was needed in the soil, and more.

It was based on the philosophy of the garden in northern Scotland called Findhorn. I had met Peter Caddy, the founder of Findhorn, while in London and was familiar with the principles. Plus, Frank had lived at Findhorn before he met me, and he had told me how wonderful it was to be around people who thought plants had intelligence.

A very special man was invited from England to come spend time at the Fondation Soleil and look after all the trees on the five estates. His name was Jim Hipkiss, and he knew how to listen to the trees on a particular property and learn which trees were in charge of the whole area. You could call him a tree whisperer.

I used to take walks with Jim, and he would point out a large majestic tree that stood at the edge of a field. By the way the tree held up its limbs, he could tell if that tree was the Grandfather of the whole field. He would advise the arborists not to fell or chop down that particular tree, because it would upset the hierarchy and balance amongst the other trees.

Jim would point out the Grandmother and the offspring. It was okay to fell one of the cousins, nieces, or nephews but never one of the stately proud strong tall trees. They held a spell over the estate, and to upset that tree was to invite disease to the others.

During our walks, Jim would ask me which tree I thought was the Grandfather. After a while, I got a sense of what he meant and started to pay attention whenever I walked in the woods or in a park near a city. I always found a majestic tree and would wink at it!

Dr. Schaller and his wife Françoise were two of the people who came to see me for individual bodywork sessions. Before a session, the doctor would tell me where his body hurt, i.e., on his right shoulder.

He suggested that I sit quietly, at the head of the table, and wait until I had a feeling of what kind of treatment to give. He encouraged me to trust the images and intuitive guidance I was given.

He said that perhaps I wouldn't touch his right shoulder at all or perhaps briefly. In any case, he said that by following my intuition, I would be led to what to do next.

Apparently, the doctor had watched me give classes and paid attention to how I phrased my knowledge. I was very *proud* of what I knew. If a student asked me about reflexology and I was teaching Polarity at the time, I would proudly say, "Well, I'll be teaching that next weekend, and I'll answer it then."

I was so rigid and kept the different techniques and methods separate. I did not know how to blend all the skills I had and allow for a more spatial creative expression. But Dr. Schaller had an idea how to loosen me up, and it worked.

Each time he came for a session, he asked me to sit quietly at the head of the table and not do any form of massage until I had the intuitive feeling to do it. Well, sometimes I waited much longer than was comfortable. I had to *do* something.

He was allowing me to *be* in the moment. That's a very different approach. It's moving from the duality realm into the non-duality realm.

That shift took place over the next year and a half. It was not sudden, but gradual. I first knew something was shifting when I began to have strange sensations in my head. I was not sure what was actually happening, yet I heard loud cracking noises in my skull.

I would be giving a session, moving my hands here and there allowing intuition to guide me, and then a quick loud sound, like a crack, would bellow throughout my brain. A few seconds later, my mind would be more expansive, like tumbling into an arena of more possibilities.

Sometimes the doctor came to see me four times a week. Each time, I sat quietly before the session and then followed my intuitive notions, and the snaps and groans and ledges of my brain would shift, move, and make more space.

Time after time, I would have a vast expansive awareness of all the techniques of bodywork that I had studied. I began to superimpose the chart of Touch for Health onto the zones of reflexology and then onto the electromagnetic pathways and chakras in the human body that I knew through polarity therapy. In this way, I could *see* how all the therapies interacted with one another.

I went from compartmentalizing what I knew to *knowing*, as wisdom, what I knew. While I gave massages to the Schallers and the staff, I went into the theta realm. At some point, a trickle of an idea of which technique to use would pop into my mind, as clear as day.

I was able to sit quietly and wait, then allow the inspiration to come pouring in. A spherical map of all the different modalities — pressure points, meridians, muscle insertions and origins, tight muscle fibers, reflexology — often appeared in my mind. Each person had his or her own map, and I trusted it.

And of course I became more flexible when a student asked any question in my classes, and I was able to see the relevance and answer accordingly.

Life started to become spherical rather than linear, and more and more I understood the meaning behind the concept of holistic health and the mind, body, and spirit connections.

CHAPTER 8

Beings around the Great Table

I matured a great deal while I stayed at the Schallers's in Geneva. I had gone through my own quantum leap in my approach to bodywork. Also, my contemplation on how beneficial relaxation was, continued to incubate.

It felt right to say goodbye to the Schallers, the staff, and to Fondation Soleil. We would catch up with them in a few more years but under different circumstances.

Frank and I wanted a vacation so we headed southeast to India, Bali, and Fiji for three months. It took me one whole month to stop asking people what time it was. I finally got into the flow of nonlinear and non-duality living, and loved it.

After the vacation, we were invited to teach at the New South Wales College of Osteopathy and Natural Therapeutics in Sydney, Australia. After that, the Aio-Wira Yoga Center outside the city of Auckland, New Zealand, invited us to teach there. It was while we were in Sydney that we were invited to teach in Perth, on the other side of the country, and I shared how we found a house for our six-month stay back in Chapter 1. Those were remarkable years, and I blossomed.

After eight years of travel, we returned to the United States. Frank decided he preferred to live in Sydney so he returned to Australia and ended up living there for the rest of his life. I remained in the States and worked as a massage therapist in San Diego and in Maine.

Two weeks after he left, I was rear-ended by a reckless driver and got a whiplash. Bummer. It hurt so much to give massages.

While I convalesced I had a most valuable vision — one I call "Beings around the Great Table." Remember that I had not received a vision since 1977 when the Temple of the Emerald Green Water was shown to me while in Geneva. It was now 1985, my companion had just left, and I was living alone for the first time in eight years. I believe this next vision came to me because I needed spiritual support. Here's what happened:

I was resting my sore neck from the whiplash injury. The sunlight shone through the sheer curtains near my bed. I was enjoying the soft light when I *saw* a big white puffy cloud come through the window, right into the room. Out of the cloud came a fully extended arm with a wide open hand on the end. This extended arm continued to move out of the cloud until it was very near to me.

The hand moved towards me and attached itself, like a suction cup, to my forehead. The suction pulled my astral body out of my physical body, and I was gently pulled out of my bed, out of the window, and out across space and time.

It was like moving swiftly through a stream of rushing water that was full of air, and I was going upstream watching the air-like quality of water flowing to either side of my face. I saw many colored streams of light. Colors like robin-egg blue and sunlight yellow, with some pastel rose and touches of iris violet, flowed past my eyes.

Gradually there were no more colored lights, and I came upon a large white cloud. I moved inside the cloud and saw a room that had no walls.

In the middle of the room, there was a large oblong table that looked like a dining table, made out of dark walnut-like wood. It was very grand, and there were twelve chairs placed around it — a chair was on each end of the table and five along each side.

Gradually, Beings came into view, and I saw that they were all seated around the table. There were eleven Beings in all, which meant that one of the chairs was empty. The Being at the end of the table reached over, moved the empty chair out from the table, and motioned for me to sit down. I did and looked up to see them all. They were all dressed in robes made out of a light blue linen fabric with gold trim around the edges of the sleeves. The gold trim shimmered with a scintillating glow.

I noticed the gentle Being sitting at the far end of the table, and this Being nodded to me. I could see the face: It was aged and venerable and very kind. It was neither male nor female, yet a living entity that was whole in mind, body, and spirit.

To my right were four Beings sitting along the side of me, and on the opposite side of the table were five Beings, all sitting. I could not see their faces, more like a subtle outline of a face. The only face I could make out was the venerable Ancient One at the end of the table.

This Being spoke to me and said, *We are glad you are here. This is where you came from, and we are your family. You can come here for anything you need, and we will help you.*

I took this in stride, as if I was expecting this and sat a while at this great table. I felt very safe and secure. I was in an altered state and could not think of anything to ask. I already knew everything. There was no lack. I was glad to be there. The feeling of belonging seeped into me, and I beamed with thankfulness.

As I nodded thank you, I swished back to where I was relaxing, opened my eyes, and just stayed there, astounded with the experience.

Over the years, I have been able to revisit these grand Beings sitting around the table. Occasionally I can make out some of the faces, but most of the time the faces are subtle except for the gentle Ancient One at the far end of the table.

I feel so at home with them all. I go there and just sit and be with them, enjoying the loud silence and great surge of inner peace.

I do not receive words or advice, rather a presence of good will and unconditional love. Even as I write this I can feel the strength and courage I receive from knowing they are there, just beyond time and space — a puffy white cloud away. I have named this experience the Beings around the Great Table.

Since I have begun doing theta patterning, I have energetically taken some clients to this place of the Great Table. It is all on the subtle planes. Most of the time the Beings hum and make low sounds that are soothing. One time I energetically laid a woman on the Great Table, and the Beings put their hands on her. There was a strong electric charge of good will.

She did tell me later that she felt deep inner calmness.

CHAPTER 9

The Crystal Cave

Shortly thereafter, just three years after being shown the Beings around the Great Table, I was given another vision, one that I use for helping other people.

I had moved to Camden, Maine, and was working at a very posh health spa named Europa Salon.

It was August 1988 and a beautiful summer night. There was a full moon, and a group of women, myself included, decided to get together and celebrate by making a medicine wheel.

We all met at a cottage on Alfred Lake, just outside of town. There were five of us, and we sat in a circle on the floor. We could see the moon outside. It was rising up over the hills, and its reflection shone back across the water. It was magical.

The woman doing the medicine wheel was a friend, Cynthia, and she lit the candle facing to the east and called in the direction:

"Let the eagle in the East bring in new beginnings."

With the lighting of the next candle, she called in the South:

"May the humble mouse in the direction of the South bring us light, warmth, and tenderness.

"May the bear in the West give us strength and stamina to keep going, no matter what!" She gave an emphasis on *what* and lit the candle.

"Let the white buffalo in the North guide the way to our true spirit."

All five of us placed a small token in the circle for a blessing and settled in for a meditation. Cynthia put on a cassette tape, and eerie music started to play.

I felt a presence touch my hand. A guide I had met before was standing there, in front of me, only he was about six inches off the floor. He was an aborigine and was wearing just a loin cloth. His hair was matted, and he held a staff in his right hand. It had been a few years since I had seen him. I had always called him Yahn.

The music played in the background, and all four of the other women were in their own world. I obviously was in mine! Yahn tugged on my hand and cocked his head as if to say, *Come on, I want to take you somewhere.*

I allowed the tug to pull me out of my body and floated up out the window, gradually lifting higher and higher over the ground. We were now over the lake, about 100 feet in the air, flying along the reflection of the moon path. I looked over at Yahn and said, *How do I know if I can get back?*

Go back now, he said softly. *I'll wait for you.*

Immediately I was back in the cottage, sitting on the floor. All seemed well. I thought of Yahn and was right back by his side. We lifted higher and higher, until we were far away from the Earth. It seemed like we were sky-sailing for the moon.

Once again I had doubts. *How do I know I'm safe?* I asked.

Yahn smiled at me and nodded his head towards his right, *Look over there.*

When I looked I saw Pegasus flying alongside us. I loved Pegasus and had always felt safe when he was near. (Remember Pegasus from the Emerald Green River.) Pegasus joined us, and we three zoomed upwards and forwards, through space and time, moving along swiftly.

We reached the surface of what seemed to be a small planet covered with sand, gravel, and small rocks.

Pegasus and Yahn settled down easily on the ground surface, and I followed close behind.

Pegasus pawed the surface of the ground, and we saw the outline of a trap door. Yahn bent down and wiped away the sand, exposing a large handle to open the door.

Yahn said, *Pegasus, you stay here and keep watch, and Deborah and I will go inside.*

Pegasus nodded, and Yahn lifted the door. A wide marble descending staircase wound down, deeper and deeper into the ground. Yahn and I started down. Yahn seemed to know the way and held out his hand for me. I allowed him to lead me, slowly, down the staircase.

As my eyes adjusted to the light, I saw jagged shapes of rock on the upper ceiling of what looked like a vast spacious cave. The rocks sparkled, and soon I saw that they were large crystals hanging from the ceiling: cobalt blue… the whole ceiling was a deep shade of blue.

Lowering further to the bottom of the stairs, we entered the cave. All around me was the color of cobalt blue. The walls and ceiling were covered with crystals. The floor, about the size of a football field, was shiny and smooth made out of cobalt blue marble.

In the far edge of the cave was a platform, made out of dark wood, possibly walnut. On top of the platform sat a large oversized chair with huge armrests and a ten-foot-tall backrest that made it look quite regal.

A woman sat in the chair. She wore a cape that spread out over the platform onto the marble floor. I could see speckles of twinkling lights, like stars, all over the cape. The hood framed her face.

Yahn encouraged me to walk closer to her and held my arm as we stood in front of her. The woman was a mythical creature in a woman's body. I knew she was magical and bigger than life.

I stood there, in front of the chair, and waited for what would happen. The woman (I never heard her name) reached out to me with her extended arm. Even though it did not reach me, I felt its energy in the air.

My body started to move on its own. I became straight and stiff as a board, so that I was hanging in midair, parallel to the floor. A gurney appeared and slid underneath me. My body relaxed, and I lay on top of it. It was very comfortable.

From the ceiling, a bell jar came down and gently fit over my body, and I was encased in this large piece of glass. I felt totally relaxed and safe.

The woman reached over and placed her hand on top of the bell jar. Rays of pink light came out of her hand. The pink light flowed over the bell jar, permeating all the way through the glass. I was now covered with pink light. I felt it in every cell in my body. All I could think of was that she had covered me with love.

The thought, *If ever I needed love I'll come back here to this magical lady*, went through my mind. Then, gradually, she removed her hand; the bell jar lifted up to the ceiling. The gurney was rolled away, and I was standing up straight again.

Yahn stepped forward, bowed to the woman, and held my arm. He gently led me back to the marble staircase, and we ascended to the surface.

Pegasus greeted us with smiles, Yahn smoothed the ground around the trapdoor, and we flew back to the cottage on Alfred Lake.

My astral body entered the room just as the last phrase of the music played on the tape player. I looked around the room at the four other women. Wow, had I been in another realm, or what!

I could not talk about this adventure. It was too new. I was very quiet the rest of the evening and left early to go home to bed.

The next day, I went to work at Europa Salon, and I had a new client, a woman who was visiting from New York City. She wore several large rings on her fingers and diamond earrings, and chose to keep them on. She said she was very tired and needed a massage.

She got on the table, and I started putting the oil on her back. As soon as I touched her I thought that she needed to meet the magical lady in the crystal cave! I visualized calling on Yahn, Pegasus, and the magical lady in the blue cape. Immediately, my client and I were in the crystal cave in front of the huge chair.

The gurney was rolled out, and we both were put onto it. A large bell jar was lowered, and it covered us. The mystical lady placed her hand on top of the bell jar, just like she had done the night before, and we were bathed in pink light.

I felt the love coming through during the whole massage, about an hour long. When I finished, I stood back from the table, and the woman got up and looked at me with astonishment in her eyes.

"Do you have any idea what just happened to me?" It wasn't a question but rather a statement of her experience. She looked pleased yet in awe. I very calmly placed a large fluffy white terrycloth robe around her shoulders and said I was glad she could relax.

"Well, I've never had an experience like that before." She looked quite restful and at peace. I respectively waited for her to share anything more, yet she remained silent. We looked into each other's eyes and smiled.

As she was leaving, she reached out for my arm and said, "Thank you." I nodded knowingly.

So now I had the Temple, the Emerald Green Water, the Beings around the Great Table, and now this — the Crystal Cave and the pink light that poured out love, pure spiritual love. I was in awe, like the woman I had just massaged.

Over the next several months, I returned to the Crystal Cave whenever I felt low and would ask to be put on the gurney and receive the pink light. It always made me feel better.

In one more year, I would come to know this woman, this magical woman in the Crystal Cave as a real person. She was Swami Chidvilasananda, affectionately called Gurumayi, of the Siddha Yoga tradition.

CHAPTER 10

Shaktipat

FEBRUARY 27, 1989. I will always remember that date. It was the day I received a blessing (or touch) of grace, called *shaktipat*, by a great meditation master.

I had been living and working in Camden for a full year. I wanted to see my family, so I flew out to San Diego to visit my mom and sister Judith. During the visit, the meditation center that Judith attended was offering a weekend course, and she invited me to take it with her.

When we arrived at the meditation center, I saw photographs of the meditation master, a guru named Swami Chidvilasananda — this name means play of consciousness. The affectionate name given to this swami was Gurumayi. Something about Gurumayi's face was familiar, yet I couldn't quite make it out.

Gurumayi was not there in person, and the course was taught by a traveling group of Siddha Yoga teachers. What I found out was that, even though Gurumayi was not there, she showed up energetically on the subtle planes.

During the first meditation on Saturday morning, I sat in the lotus position, repeating the mantra Om Namah Shivaya, when the guru's face appeared before me. In my mind's eye, I saw her outstretched hand reach for me.

I want to take you somewhere, I heard inside me. I went with no hesitation. We lifted up out of the building, over San Diego, across a vast expanse of water, and moved very fast. We flew over land and finally slowed down to settle on the slope of a hill where a small hut was perched.

The guru took me into the hut, smiled and left. I stood for a while in the hut, and noticed there were no curtains, no bench — it was bare. I shrugged my shoulders, looked down at my feet, and even they were bare. They reminded me of San Diego, and in a swish of a second, I was back in the meditation center in San Diego.

After the meditation, I mentioned this experience to a woman who had been with Gurumayi for a long time.

She said, "Oh, yes, that sounds like the hut that our guru's teacher, Swami Muktananda had. It's a good omen to be taken there. I'm happy for you."

But where had I seen Gurumayi before, I thought? That afternoon there was time to ask questions, and I asked one of the teachers, "Why is there a need to have a guru in the human form? The mere fact that this guru is in a body, means she must have the same sensual nature as any other human, therefore, how do I know that she is a true guru?"

The teacher smiled and nodded yet didn't say anything. There was a hush of silence in the room.

I continued talking, "I've always turned to Mother Nature as my true guru. Please talk to me about trusting in another human — having true faith."

The room's energy shifted. I felt everyone relax and my chest was filled with a warm glow. The teacher took a moment to answer.

"Gurumayi is not a normal person. She is here on Earth to assist people in their spiritual progress. With one blessing *(shaktipat),* she can wipe away years of heaviness. With one blessing, she can give a lightness to people. The Guru's whole life is devoted to the spiritual nature. Gurumayi is a gift, given to all of us."

The impact of his answer came into me as a wave of love that swooped through the room and flowed right into me.

"Thank you." I couldn't say anything else.

We all got up for a break, and rather than ponder over what he said, I allowed his answer to be enough.

The next morning while we were chanting and meditating, I had a sense that I lifted out of the room and was drifting over a beautiful garden. I walked around a building and there was Gurumayi, in her subtle form, sitting in a large chair in the cross-legged or lotus position. Her face was still. I was about 20 feet from her.

I stopped, turned toward her, and we looked at one another in a soft gentle manner. Then it clicked. I knew where I had seen her. Gurumayi opened her arms in a graceful flowing gesture, just like she did when I was with Yahn inside the Crystal Cave, and from her arms a soft yet brilliant golden light emanated forth. This golden light completely encapsulated me, and I felt peaceful.

And again that afternoon, while in quiet meditation, I had the strongest sensation that Gurumayi put her hands inside my chest cavity. She placed one hand under my heart organ, the other hand on top of it. Her face looked at me with such deep peace and contentment; then she rocked her hands around my heart. I felt so loved and appreciated.

I went back to my sister's for the evening. She said, "Deb, your eyes are so much more relaxed. You don't have that piercing look."

"I do feel more centered. What an experience. I felt love for everyone. Has Fran met Gurumayi?" Fran Burnett was a friend of both of ours and she had met Gurumayi's teacher, Swami Muktananda, about 20 years before. Fran had been on a spiritual journey of her own for many years. She also was a massage therapist, so I made an appointment to see her the next day.

After a short visit with Fran and catching up with everyday news, I got on the massage table. She worked on me for about two hours, during which time she released an old story from my shoulder muscles.

After the lengthy massage, Fran stepped back and sat on a chair near me. I lay on the table, feeling peaceful, grateful that I had such a dear friend in my life. That's when I saw the lights dancing before my eyes.

"Fran, do you see the lights over me?"

"No."

"Are you sure? They're so bright."

"Just relax into it," reassured Fran.

The lights swirled around my whole body and as the lights grew, the threads of light turned into shimmering silk-like pieces of threads that completely encased my body in the shape of a cocoon. A space was left open at the top of my head.

"Don't you see the lights?"

"No, dear, this one is for you."

Without any further ado, a deep boiling, rumbling fire exploded at the base of my spine. It was inside my body where the first chakra abides, in and around the sitting bone — the coccyx.

This ball of rumbling fire exploded! I heard a huge bang, and a loud rush of energy came moving up my inner spine, inside my body, and before I could count to three, I was propelled out the top of my head, out the window behind me, up over San Diego County, out over California. I was moving very fast.

I somehow turned to look back to where I was, and I could see the Earth, the size of a grapefruit, receding away from me. I felt safe and secure. I watched the planets in our solar system pass by, and then the Milky Way became dimmer and dimmer, and I continued propelling into outer space. Another galaxy went by — then another. I watched five galaxies go by me — or rather, I was going by them!

Finally, I slowed down and ended up in a huge vast expanse of space. I looked up: There was nothing. I looked down: There was nothing. I looked to the right: There was nothing. I looked to the left: There was nothing. There was nothing everywhere.

I was vast, with light years of clear vision. I was peaceful and calm. I felt deep joy.

There was a glimmer of light shining in the far off distance, and an arc of bright light appeared in the faraway horizon. On top of this arc of light, I saw a small shape of a sitting Buddha-like man. He was sitting in the lotus position, had a round tummy, and was laughing. The laughter traveled across endless space, like waves of undulating music, filling every corner. The laughter permeated me and filled all my cells with joy.

I had the notion that I could move freely in this new space. I threw back my hands and easily floated backwards in a flip. My right arm moved to the right, and my whole body gracefully swung to the right. I moved, like a trained gymnast, in the vast space. I was ecstatic.

Fran's face popped into my head. *Oh, Fran*, I thought. *Go back and tell Fran.* I thought of the massage table and immediately returned to Fran's room. She was still sitting on her chair.

"Oh, Fran. Oh, Fran. The lights." That's all I could say. I closed my eyes and went back to the open space.

I continued to move freely. I had miles of space to move, and I made circles that sometimes were a whole mile in circumference. I was so happy and free.

I thought of Fran again and returned to the room.

"Fran." I was silent while I just lay there on the table. "I'm going back."

After I had been in the open space for a while longer, I decided to return to the table and stay there. I knew that I would always have this as a reality experience. Nothing could take away the experience of freedom and joy that moved through my cells. I was full of bliss.

I returned to the room, opened up my eyes, gently stretched my arms, and slowly sat up, dangling my legs over the side of the table. Fran came over and brushed my shoulders and arms, kissing me on the side of my face.

I smiled and said, "Well, I'm not coming back so I might as well get up."

I moved slowly, and by the time I got out into the living room, Fran had put lunch on the dining room table.

"Here, sit down and have some soup."

"Okay." I moved slowly and sat down.

"I made this soup yesterday."

"Hmm. It's good."

The two of us sat there, quietly eating the bread and soup.

Fran's dog Toto walked over and licked my hand. Fran reached down and patted her. We looked at one another and smiled. She did not ask me about the experience, nor did I tell her.

An hour or so later, I had to leave and drive back to my mom's house, about 40 miles away, and I would be driving in rush-hour traffic.

My mind was blown and I said, "Oh dear, I don't know if I can drive."

"I have just the thing." Fran popped up from her chair and went into the other room. She carried out a large silver bowl and held it in front of me. I looked in and saw about 50 little pieces of candies individually tied up with either gold or silver foil.

"The last time I was in Mexico, I bought all these chocolates. Here take one. You know, Muktananda used to tell us that when you go way out during meditation, chocolates will bring you back. Just a little piece — you don't need much." Fran knew just what to do.

I reached in the bowl, chose a candy in gold foil and put it in my mouth. As soon as I took one or two bites, suddenly, I heard two claps of thunder, like two loud bangs inside my head. I was immediately back inside my body, totally present.

"Yes, I know how to drive. I can do this. Thank you, Fran. Goodbye."

I picked up my purse and with keys in hand, walked out to the car. I felt like I was floating on air, as if in a trance. I started the car, backed up, and drove out onto the highway.

Once I got on the freeway, I settled in at 55 miles per hour and cruised along. Not one car came up close behind me, nor did I ever have to pass a car while driving all the way down the mountain, through the valley, onto Highway 5, and the coastline to my mom's house. It was one of the easiest drives I had ever done. Effortless.

I drove up to my mom's house and parked the car. I walked into the house and saw my mom standing in the middle of the room, holding a pile of magazines in her arms.

She looked at me, gasped, dropped her magazines all over the floor and stood there, saying, "Debbie, oh Debbie."

I walked towards her, took her hands and said, "I know, Mom." We automatically walked over to the couch, and she reached for my hands again. "Oh, Debbie, I'm so happy for you."

"I'm happy too, Mom."

The two of us sat there, unable to speak. We sat there for about a half-hour, when I began to feel sleepy. I put my head in her lap, stretched out on the couch, and fell asleep while she patted my head.

We never talked about this event, yet I felt we both knew it was special.

The next day I flew back to Maine. My mind was blown. I had received visions before, but none of them was as strong and powerful as this one.

Over the next few weeks, I socialized with people I knew, yet something was missing — the harmony was gone. Maybe it had never been there before, and I just had not noticed it. I remembered Dr. Schaller advising me *to notice what you notice.*

I yearned to have time to be quiet, to reflect, and to integrate what had happened. I had been given a spiritual awakening and was going through a spiritual cleansing, and my priorities had changed. I had made a quantum leap in my resonating vibrational frequency. I was changed both inside and outside.

It took about three years to digest and integrate all these changes. I was single during that time, and finally I knew I was ready to be in another relationship.

But who and what would he be like? Did I have a say in the matter? Could I do theta patterning and attract him? I decided to give it a try.

CHAPTER 11

Our Beech Hill Home

I had a good life in Maine and was ready to share it with someone. The spiritual experiences put a deep contentment in my soul, and I was happy. Because of that, I believed I was ready to be in a relationship where both of us could be ourselves, with respect for the other.

I thought long and hard about what kind of life partner I would like, and in about a month I was ready to go into deep relaxation and do the theta patterning. I was excited and felt uplifted about the project. I wrote a list of his qualities and put it into present tense to act as if it had already happened.

He is near my age.

He is really happy with me, loves me, and enjoys who I am.

I adore and love him, and we laugh together.

He likes to be outside, an outdoorsman going canoeing and camping.

He likes to fix things around the house.

He has his own life interests as I have my own. He is secure in himself; we are both independent, and at the same time we like to share a deep sense of togetherness.

We are bonded. We are tight. It's like a home with two pillars: I am on one side and he on the other. It appears we are different, and yet we have a deep connection.

He is the right height for me, in good health, has a healthy financial approach, and is respected by the community. We look good together.

We share a similar philosophy.

And he loves Maine.

I repeated theta patterning several times over the next couple of months. Each time I did the process I filled my heart with love, spilled love all over the list of intentions, and ended each session in the Crystal Cave, under the bell jar with love pouring down on me. And then I let it go, over and over again.

Four years passed.

Then the inevitable magic moment in time arrived. I walked from a lit room into a dark room, and there was a man sitting in the dark who saw me. He said I was lit up and knew he wanted to get to know me. It's so curious to me how walking from one room into another can change everything. It helps to be lit up from behind! His name was Edgar Frederick Eaton, Jr., and he lived about two hours away, over in the western part of Maine. He was a registered Maine Guide, and he took people on canoe trips down many of the rivers in Maine.

He described one trip down the St. Croix River, which is part of the border between Maine and New Brunswick, Canada. I could see myself sitting in a canoe, paddling down the river, and breathing in the fresh air. I asked if there was a chance I could go on one of the canoe trips, and he assured me that I could go along.

It was such a joy to be with Ed. He was so at home with himself, and I sensed he went into theta easily. He wanted to make sure that I was comfortable with camping and canoeing, so over the 4th of July that first year, he took me to the far eastern part of Maine for a four day canoe trip. That's a great way to learn about someone.

He took care of everything. All I had to do was be there and paddle. Ed matched all the qualities on my list, and luckily I was his choice of partner as well. He proposed to me on that canoe trip, and we were married a year later in the small coastal town of Camden.

Where were we going to live? I had definite ideas and put those into the theta patterning process. I drew a picture of a wraparound driveway ending at the entrance to a small house. The land around the house had flower gardens, and there was a sunny spot for the vegetable garden. I drew water pools, a small brook, and an overall ambiance of contentment. I imagined about six acres and *saw* the land, trees, and surrounding environment in a natural pleasant setting. Ed and I hoped to live near the hub center of Belfast, a small town on the Penobscot Bay in Waldo County, yet the house and land held priority.

It took us about one year to find the place. Actually, Ed found it on the internet and showed it to me. At first I turned it down, because the house was too small.

A couple of months later, after looking for houses all over Waldo County, I had a dream. In the dream, the three gurus I had grown to love (Bhagawan Nityananda, the guru who was in the vast space when I received shaktipat, Muktananda, and Gurumayi) approached me and crooked their fingers at me as if to say, *come on with us*. In the dream, the three of them floated over the property I had just negated. They were holding hands, floating about a foot above the ground, and laughing.

When I woke up, I shrugged my shoulders and did not pay any attention to the dream. The next night I had the same dream! The three of them showed up, beckoned me to follow them, took my hand, and flew me over the property. Okay, I got it! Ed and I made an offer, and in three days it was accepted.

We had lived there a few days when I was outside unpacking the car. My back was to the house, and a strange prickly feeling crawled up my back. I turned around with a start and looked right into a tree on the edge of the property.

It was a huge white pine tree, majestic and tall, similar to the white pine tree I had sat under as a child. I *knew* it was the Grandfather Tree of the property. I remembered what the tree whisperer, Jim Hipkiss, had taught me about honoring the tree's presence.

As I looked at the trunk of the tree, I could make out two big droopy eyes where two limbs used to be, like an elephant's. A tree limb was missing right where an elephant's trunk could have been, and it looked like a small pug nose; a small gash near the base made a perfect place for a mouth. There was a face on the trunk!

"Oh, so you're why we're here! Hi, nice to meet you. I'm going to name you Ganesh." Ganesh is the Hindu god for clearing away obstacles, and he seemed perfect for this property that was slowly becoming Ed's and mine.

The property is precious to us. We have made it our home. I have a combined vegetable, herb, and flower garden, where I practice the principles of organic gardening and invite the nature spirits to come, similar to the Findhorn Garden in northern Scotland.

I have made five major compost piles in different areas around the six acres and turn them over and over again to make soil and mulch dressings for next year's soil. I love making soil; it's like being connected to all life. The soil in the gardens is rich, healthy, and full of worms.

I was outside by the compost pile one day and was using the pitch fork to turn the pile when I *felt* I was being watched. I stopped, looked around, and could not see anything or anybody. So I continued turning the pile when once again, there was the strongest *feeling* that a presence was near.

I looked around and out of the corner of my eye I *sensed* the form of a small person. I stated out loud that I was comfortable in seeing the presence and that I was agreeable to communicate. Would that be all right?

I *saw* (in my mind's eye) a nature spirit materialize on the high point of land at the edge of the woods. He had a slightly more masculine energy than a feminine one, and he was about four feet tall wearing a linen beige shirt with pale green trousers that went just below his knees. His hair was light brown and was shaped around his small face like a Dutch boy. Everything about him was sweet, benign, and tender.

I felt tenderness in my heart and said "Hi, I can see you. I am so glad you let me see you. What's your name?"

I heard his answer intuitively. "Odin."

"Hi, Odin, how are you? How old are you and how long have you lived here?"

"I have lived here over 700 years, and the nature spirits and I want to tell you that we are pleased how well the two of you are taking care of this land. Thank you."

"Oh my goodness, how wonderful to hear that. Odin, would you be willing to help me garden?" I held my breath in anticipation, because to have the help of a nature spirit while gardening is a sure sign of success.

"Yes, I'll help you. Just call out my name, wait for inspiration, and follow the ideas that pop into your head." And with that, he gradually faded back into his vibratory realm. Ever since then, I start my gardening chores with a request for his help. Is that why the vegetables have been so delicious these last few years?

One of the days I was outside gardening, I was impressed with the presence of all the nature spirits in the area. It felt full of a pulsating awareness.

In a flash of light, all three of the inner guides I had known since I was five, flew out of my energetic body. I *saw* three wisps of grey smoke lift up and drift out of my body and sail over the landscape as if they were floating on the breeze. And then I was alone. Alone. I did not have any spirits in my energy field. So this is what it feels like to be solo.

The next time a client came to see me for a massage, I definitely felt the absence of the three spirits. I had always thought I worked with a *spirit team* and often said to the client that *we'll see what we can do* when they told me a problem. That was no longer the case — I did not feel any enthusiasm when I massaged her. Sure, I knew the bodywork techniques and how to give a massage. What was lacking was my depth of interest in how everything was all connected together in her mind, body, and spirit.

I lost interest. I also lost all my clients due to a lack of interest, on my part and on theirs'. It was uncanny. That was in November of 2011. I had been offering massage and bodywork since 1972 — a total of 39 years.

I gave my massage table away, sorted through countless books on bodywork that had sat on my bookshelves for years, and gave them to the library.

I wondered what was next. I was about to find out.

CHAPTER 12

The Blue Beings

On Sunday morning at 9:50 AM, February 26, 2012, a few months after the spirit guides had left my energy field, I was standing in my kitchen getting ready to do some chores around the house. The strangest thing happened: An invisible wall of dense energy was directly in front of me. It was so real that I could not move in any direction. I received the thought, *Now — right this minute — go lie down and drop into deep relaxation.* I left the kitchen, and lay down to become quiet. What was going to happen?

I lay down, closed my eyes, and in one hour's time I opened my eyes again. In that hour, I was shown, in great detail, a vision to help cleanse and purify myself and others. I had not received a vision since 1988, a 24-year span, when I was shown the Crystal Cave.

As soon as I closed my eyes, in just a few seconds, I felt myself tumble down, down, down into a deeper quiet place within me. It felt like I was falling down, further and further through the layers of the Earth. I found myself in a place so deep and quiet that I could not hear the sounds of the day nor see the glow of the natural light.

All was very still.

I arrived at the same place that I have visited for years in my deep relaxation journeys. It is a place very deep within the Earth. The landscape changes from large open spaces with ledges on which to sit, to a winding footpath that meanders alongside a small brook. I have always been able to feel the mist that rises from the babbling brook and have enjoyed looking at the natural flora growing alongside it.

There is a nature spirit with a male energy who guards the footpath. I have named him Gog, (I have no idea why). Over the years, I have often visited him — just sitting beside him and absorbing the natural settings. So on this day in February, I was here again, via the message to go now into deep relaxation.

This time when I saw Gog, he took my hand — something he had not done before — and led me further down the footpath. This was the first time I had gone beyond the babbling brook. He guided me around a curve in the path, and there were two ethereal beings standing right there, in the path.

Gog introduced me to the two beings, as if he were presenting me to royalty. I had never seen the likes of them before. They were very tall and they did not have any faces that I could see. What I could see was that they were clad in blue cloaks, a clear robin-egg blue that covered them from head to toe. Gog looked at me as if to say, *you're in good hands now,* and left to return to guard the footpath.

One of these beings reached out and escorted me through a doorway. On the other side of the door was a cavern; it looked like a dungeon and fell even deeper into the middle of the Earth. If I could have smelled it, the odor would have been dank and musty. The tall beings invited me to come to the rim of the cavern and look down. As I peered into the deep hole, I could see a pile of mangled bodies. The bodies were alive yet groaned and moaned in extreme discomfort. I saw arms and elbows that were swollen with open sores on the rest of their bodies.

I cringed and stepped back away from the rim and said "No, I don't like to see that."

The two beings had a glow of blue light around them, then smiled and pointed up to my right. "Look up there."

As I turned my head, I became aware of a shaft of scintillating light that began where we three were standing. The light was moving up, higher and higher, traveling thousands of miles up into outer space. The light was like a round beam of a laser that was just wide enough for my body to easily fit inside.

I stepped into it and was slowly propelled towards the upper area of space. I lifted up higher and higher along this beam of light, moving towards a brilliant collection of sunbeams.

At the top of the beam of light I *saw* the group of beings that I met around the great table. All eleven of them were there, greeting me. I was so glad to see them. They were like my spiritual family. They were very happy to see me too, and motioned me to come closer and see what was there, just ahead.

It was a platform of floating space, a place where I could easily stand, and yet there was no sense of any grounding or earthlike substance around the area. It felt like an endless space of warm light that existed for an eternity.

In the center of this platform was a large opening upwards to the sky, and light poured through it. It poured down on the platform, like a cosmic shower head. As I stood underneath this cosmic shower head, a cascade of swirling, shining yellow, pink, blue, lilac, soft green, and pearly white light swirled and poured out of the shower, bathing my whole body.

The group of beings, my spiritual family, said that I needed to have my tiredness bathed away. I stood there and thoroughly accepted this stream-of-light bath. After I was cleansed and refreshed, the group of beings motioned me to follow them. They pointed in the direction of the dungeon.

The laser beam was connecting the floating platform where I was standing, all the way down to the dungeon where the mangled bodies were gathered. The group of beings then moved their arms over their heads and made circular motions — and just like that, an escalator (a running walkway) magically appeared and connected the two polarized ends. The escalator was in the shape of a figure eight, the infinity symbol, and it moved back and forth from the platform to the dungeon.

So now I could see the laser beam, the moving infinity symbol, the dungeon, and the cosmic shower! All connected, and everything was in motion with a high frequency vibration.

At that point, the group of beings signaled me to follow them, and they positioned themselves all along the escalator. All this time, the two Blue Beings (I decided that was their name) had remained near the dungeon.

They looked up at me, and I saw their faces — the concept of total kindness came to mind.

They reached down into the mangled pile of miserable bodies and picked up one of them. This soul, this individual, was passed from one being to another — even passed to me as I passed the individual on towards the top of the escalator. All of us worked together: We relayed the individual up to the platform. The wretched soul was gently placed under the cosmic shower head, and scintillating light of swirling colors poured all over the collapsed figure. I stood there and watched as the dirt and grime was washed off the body; then the swollen elbows and feet returned to pliable arms and legs. The open sores closed up and vanished, and the expression on this soul's face went from anguish to sweet serenity. The soul became a man or a woman, who was able to stand upright. Purification had taken place.

I had never seen anything like this before. I was so full of love, joy, and gratitude. I had a heart bursting with so many thanks, and we all started to work together again.

Now the infinity escalator was in full motion. One soul was picked up from the dungeon, and was relayed up to the cosmic shower. Over and over again, the group of beings and I relayed one soul after another and we all witnessed them receiving the cleansing from the cosmic shower. The tall Blue Beings remained near the dungeon and my spiritual family, the Great Beings, worked with me up and down the escalator.

The mixture of colors pouring out of the cosmic shower had a predominant color of gold, like golden sunlight. Therefore I have named this vision the Blue Beings and the Golden Light. Eventually, all the souls that had been huddled in the dark dungeon were picked up and lifted up to the Golden Light.

After this precious vision, I returned to my room and lay there for a while. All was calm; all was love.

This vision is so useful in changing the frequency of a person, lifting it up to a higher vibration. Since then, when I enter into theta patterning, the Blue Beings often interact with me and guide how the session needs to go. Whether I am doing a theta patterning for myself or for someone else, the Blue Beings guide me to the Temple of the Emerald Water, or to the Crystal Cave, or to the Golden Light.

These three visions offer the remarkable power of color: emerald green, pink, cobalt blue, and gold. The Blue Beings are kind and offer their help for anyone who wishes to ask for it. The last time I asked for their help, they took me to the Temple with the Emerald Water, and there on the sloped lawn the Crystal Cave and the Golden Light and escalator were all set up, ready to help any number of people and animals.

The following page has a shorter version of the Blue Beings so that you can use it when you visit your own theta realm.

The Blue Beings

1. There are two beings who are here to help: They are around 15 feet tall, very slim and smooth looking, and they wear long blue flowing robes made out of a translucent material similar to silk.

2. The Blue Beings, as they can be called, show you a shaft of scintillating light that is cascading down from outer space, from thousands of miles away.

3. The light is like a round laser beam of iridescent light that is just wide enough for your body to easily fit inside. This light can propel you, slowly, towards the upper area of space. You can be lifted higher and higher along this beam of iridescent light, moving towards a brilliant collection of golden sunbeams.

4. At the top of this beam of light, you meet your spiritual guides. They are all very happy to see you again, and they use their hands to motion you to move closer and see what is there, just ahead.

5. It is a platform of floating space, a place where you can easily stand and feel very safe and secure. It feels like an endless space of warm light that exists for an eternity.

6. In the center of this place is a large opening in the sky, and light pours through it. Light pours down on the platform, and you stand underneath this cascade of swirling, shining yellow, pink, blue, lilac, soft green, and pearly white scintillating light. It pours and swirls all over you, bathing your whole body in golden light.

7. Your tiredness is washed away. You lift up your face and receive this golden stream of light bath. It is like a cosmic shower pouring out a very large shower head.

8. You are bathed in golden streams of love pouring down from the Universe, bathing your body with unconditional love — rejuvenating all the cells in your body.

9. You receive deep rest and pure love.

10. Open your eyes and give thanks to the dear Blue Beings.

CHAPTER 13

Strengthening the Immune System

I n the 1960's when I first heard of the immune system I wondered where it was and when I found it, what would I do with it. It seemed so elusive.

I was healthy until my early 40's when I felt the absence of my immune system and started to get colds and the flu on a regular basis. I didn't have the stamina I had always depended upon and to make things worse, I had disturbing dreams waking me up in the middle of the night.

I found a good therapist who was using the technique of proprioceptive writing. This automatic writing helped me to unlock my unconscious so that I could uncover what the nightmarish dreams were trying to tell me. A childhood memory was trying to come out, be remembered and then released. I was a young girl of six years old and walked into a glen in the woods. I had walked in on four boys, all around ten years old, doing their rites-of-passage on one another. I knew all of them. Bad timing. They did NOT want me to tell on them so they pinned me down on the ground, and scared the daylights out of me.

I promised never to tell and unbeknownst to me, my immune system promised to never process this as well. It lay buried in my cells and finally, when the timing was right, my immune system started yelling and it took a while before I could interpret what it was saying. My body had to go through a big breakdown and I became very ill with Epstein - Barr virus, aka Chronic Fatigue Syndrome. That explained all the colds and flu I had been having.

To get well, I went to the Hippocrates Health Institute in West Palm Beach, Florida and stayed there for four months. During that time, I took the Health Educator Course and studied with holistic teachers and therapists who taught the mind/body connection between the acid & alkaline balance in the body.

When we experience a trauma, the body holds it as an acidic build-up in the cells. When we eat alkaline foods, mainly sprouts, juices and raw foods, the body releases the acidic build-up and cellular memories are often released. During the cleanse, the immune system can perform its role and return the body, mind, and spirit back into natural balance and good health.

That's what happened to me. As I ate an alkaline diet over those four months, my body released the cellular memory and made space for me to forgive the young boys and to forgive myself for the years of being afraid.

I had found my immune system and experienced how powerful it was. It had sent me messages from my deep unconscious that something needed to be cleansed out of my cells. It also brought me to a complete stop (with the Epstein-Barr) and made me pay attention.

I believe one of the many functions of the immune system is a natural intelligence. This intelligence guides us into wellness and the ability to forgive. I believe there is no part of me that is not my immune system. It can be found everywhere and for me, it is no longer elusive.

I take a deep breath in and I am breathing in my immune system. I smile at a beautiful flower and my immune system smiles. I hold my breath and gasp with fright and my immune system is startled and possibly challenged.

I have a hunch that my immune system was preparing me for this next challenge. About ten years ago, I was gardening on a fine day in early June when a wasp, a yellow jacket, flew into my blouse and stung me on a very sensitive area of my sternum; the xiphoid process. Within a few days, my xiphoid process became hard and twisted at a right angle to the rest of my sternum. I had trouble bending over and if anything touched it, it hurt a great deal.

It was two days after I was stung when I received a phone call that my childhood friend, Sandy, a second cousin, had suffered a terrible accident; she had tripped over the vacuum cleaner cord, lost her balance, fallen down the kitchen stairs into the basement and when she landed on the cement floor, had died instantly. I was so distraught from the news that I reacted by bursting into tears over the next few weeks.

I finally went to my primary doctor and when she saw my emotional state, she suggested I go see a therapist. The one she recommended turned out to be perfect for what I needed at the time. What I realized was my father had forced me down into the basement when I was very young and had locked me in. I had memories of yelling, crying and beating on the door to let me back into the kitchen.

I also had memories of trying to crawl up into my father's lap and him pushing me away, saying he didn't love me at that moment.

All of this turmoil weakened my immune system: grieving my childhood friend, dealing with the painful wasp sting, and recalling memories of rejection from my father. My health plummeted.

Whether I received the Lyme bacteria from the wasp or from a tick bite may never be known but the Lyme bacteria took hold and within a year, my whole body was failing. My gall bladder, liver and pancreas were the organs affected. I lay in bed for three months, unable to move and at one point, I do remember a benevolent being, like Jesus, standing in the doorway. I remember acknowledging him with a nod saying I didn't have the energy to do anything. *Do what you will with me.*

I had not been to the Hippocrates Health Institute for 18 years and knew that I had to go back. As soon as I got there, I was put on massive amounts of garlic, eaten with an apple. In about one week, after eating five cloves of garlic several times a day, the bacterial infection was gone and my health rebounded. In the second week, after eating raw foods and heaps of sunflower sprouts at each meal, I started to be light and springy again. By the third week, I was once again my healthy self. I salute my immune system.

When I returned to my life here in Maine, the twisted xiphoid process was still painful and bending over was still a problem. Plus, I continued to have a mild case of pancreatitis. Both concerned me very much. I had learned that Lyme was stimulated by three factors: bacteria, environmental toxins, and emotional upsets. I had also remembered from studying the five-element theory of acupuncture that the pancreas was the organ that balanced the sweetness of life.

I began to pay attention to the times when the area near my pancreas and the twisted xiphoid process were at their most aggravated; and that was when I felt unloved in some way.

I designed a theta patterning prayer specifically for my pancreas and my xiphoid. I would drop deep into theta and when I breathed in I would say *I am love* and when I breathed out I would say *I am light.* I practiced doing the 3 * 2* 1* exercises (explained in Chapter Three) almost daily and for a couple of years, I did my best to notice how I received love and how I rejected it at the same time.

I have learned that for me, receiving love is more awkward than giving love. When I hear of people having trouble with their pancreas I have a great deal of compassion for them because it is an on-going learning about the giving and receiving of love.

To strengthen the immune system, I have found deep relaxation to be of great importance. When I drop into theta and invite the emerald green waters to pour into me, I feel my immune system becoming stronger. Each time I invite the golden rays of light the Blue Beings showed me, I feel my immune system becoming stronger. I believe by 2013, when I had the mystical experience with the breath of God, my immune system was able to integrate the receiving of love from the divine source. I hold the breath of God within me as a sublime miracle.

I now feel connected to all parts of myself; therefore I feel that I am one with my immune system. It is now easy for me to explain complicated concepts in a simple manner. I have always thought that life was simple if we understood how the ego and the spiritual side of our nature wove together. To put it simply, we are human beings — humans with an ego — and beings of spirit.

The following is a list of my beliefs that I feel strengthen the immune system.

The quantum theory helps to explain when we, as humans, are ready for the next step in our lives.

The unified field theory helps to explain how the transformation attracts people and events so that it all can happen.

The duality stage of consciousness is using the human ego side of our nature; the non-duality is engaging with our spiritual nature.

I believe it is a natural state for people to have visions, hear messages, and feel impressions.

I believe that the spirit lives within us, as us, in our being.

I believe that the human brain/mind, in its entirety, is conscious and aware of the expanded universe. It is like a filter that goes from the all-knowing and squeezes down into a small portion so that we humans can function as individuals without becoming overwhelmed with the information from the universe. It would be a bit much!

I believe that on occasion, most people have an experience when the filter of the brain/mind readjusts, and some of the all-knowing from the universe pours into the small portion that they are familiar with. Although that exposure may be only for a moment, it wakes them up to their own divinity and can have an everlasting effect on their lives.

I believe that the most prominent vibration in the universe is love. Love is a vibration that *is*. Love is a state of *being*.

I believe that positivity is stronger than negativity.

I believe that a focused thought of good will with the intention of love is the strongest force in the universe. I believe that this force is connected to our immune system, and we can tap into that force.

In my life now, I teach people how to go into deep relaxation and do their own theta patterning. If someone feels a need for extra help, I offer them a theta patterning that I do on my own and *send* it to them from a distance, no matter how far away they are.

While I am doing theta patterning, I go to the inner realms of the Temple with the Emerald Water, the Crystal Cave, and the Blue Beings. Over time, all these inner realms have merged into one, and I now go to the lawn at the Temple and interact with all the visions I've described. It's like being at a health fair in the spirit realms. I explain all this as part of the unified field theory. It's amazing, isn't it!

I continue to be amazed at the small things in life; when I was in my late 20's, I went into a grocery store, to the produce section. I noticed an elderly woman holding a head of lettuce in her hand. Something about the way she was holding it caught my eye. I watched her, and from 20 feet away I could feel her intense appreciation for the lettuce. She was in the moment and in love with it. I walked over to her, stood next to her until she noticed me. I leaned in and said, "It's fun, isn't it!"

"Oh yes, it is!" She replied.

About the Author

Deborah Knight Eaton was born and raised in rural Maine. At the early age of eleven, her father accepted a teaching job in San Diego, California and the whole family moved out west. As a teenager, she joined a neighborhood community center and met Carl Rogers, the author of *On Becoming a Person*. She attended his sensitivity groups throughout her teenage years which were her introduction into humanistic psychology.

Deborah has had a lifelong career in the healing arts and has studied and taught here in the United States, in England, Europe, Australia and in New Zealand.

In 2013, she experienced a divine intervention that she calls the breath of God (as detailed in the book). This has given her the confidence to write about her spiritual wisdom.

Deborah lives in Mid-Coast Maine with her husband, Edgar. She loves gardening, outdoor activities, writing in the wintertime and going deep into theta consciousness. She has a private practice as a Spiritual Counselor.

Theta Patterning Services

Have you been wanting to learn how to relax deeply?

Have you been wanting to learn the skill of entering the brain wave of theta and remain awake?

Are you aware that when we are in the brain wave of theta, we can heal the mind and body connection and co-create the future?

Every time we fall asleep, we enter the theta brain wave. This is our birthright. When we relax deeply and enter theta, but *remain awake and alert,* we can develop a healthy body-mind-spirit pattern, heal our past, and create our future.

I call this approach **theta patterning**.

Please contact me for the following **theta patterning** services:

- **Individual Sessions** (Local or Long-Distance)
- **Self-Help Classes**
- **Teacher Training**

Please email me and we can decide what is best for you.

Deborah Knight Eaton

thetapatterning@gmail.com

Resources

The Essene Gospel of Peace **by Edmond Bordeaux Szekely**
I.B.S. International (International Biogenic Society)
P.O. Box 849 Nelson, B.C. CANADA V1L 6A5

Bhagawan Nityananda of Ganeshpuri **by Swami Muktananda Paramahamsa**
Siddha Yoga Meditation Bookstore 371 Brickman Road
South Fallsburg, NY 12779-0600, USA
(914) 434-0124

ESP (Extrasensory Perceptions) **by Susy Smith**

Findhorn Gardens
Email: enquiries@ findhorn.org

The Hippocrates Diet and Health Program **by Ann Wigmore**
Hippocrates Health Institute 1443 Palmdale Court
West Palm Beach, FL 33411 www.hippocratesinstitute.org

A Brief History of Everything **by Ken Wilbur**

The Wisdom Jesus **by Cynthia Bourgeault**

Healing for the Age of Enlightenment **by Stanley Burroughs**

Ayurveda: The Science of Self-Healing **by Dr. Vasant Lad**

Polarity Therapy: The Complete Collected Works Vol. 1 **by Randolph Stone**

The Politics of Experience **by R.D. Laing**

My Spiritual Journey **by The Dalai Lama**

Give the Gift of Relaxation

Going Deep: My Transcendent Journey into Theta Consciousness

This book is an excellent gift for someone who would like to learn the practice of deep relaxation.
Signed copies can be purchased by emailing the author: thetapatterning@gmail.com

Up and Coming Books by the Author: Deborah Knight Eaton

Deb's Prophecy: Her Mentorship with Remarkable People

Deborah takes you on her world travels and weaves her hard to learn lessons with the joys of finally understanding what it means to be a fully actualized person.

Basil, the Dragon of Route One

This is a fantasy book for the child in all of us. A joyful book full of mirth, shows us when we offer appreciation for the beauty in nature, we are blessed with all its unconditional love.

Freedom from Self-Sabotage

Deborah describes the seven steps needed to be free of resistance and how to change without sabotage getting in the way. This is a self-help workbook full of good tips.

Printed in the United States
By Bookmasters